Methuen Introductions to Development

Series Editors:
John Bale and David Drakakis-Smith

Development and Underdevelopment

In the same series

John Cole

Development and Underdevelopment

A profile of the Third World

METHUEN
London and New York

First published in 1987 by
Methuen & Co. Ltd
11 New Fetter Lane, London EC4P 4EE

Published in the USA by
Methuen & Co.
in association with Methuen, Inc.
29 West 35th Street, New York NY 10001

© 1987 J. P. Cole

Typeset by Hope Services, Abingdon, Oxon
Printed in Great Britain
by Richard Clay Ltd, Bungay, Suffolk

British Library Cataloguing in Publication Data

Cole, J. P.
Development and underdevelopment: a profile of the Third World.—(Methuen introductions to
development)
1. Developing countries—Economic conditions
I. Title
330.9172'4   HC59.7

ISBN 0-416-92080-2

Library of Congress Cataloging-in-Publication Data

Cole, J. P. (John Peter), 1928–
Development and underdevelopment.
(Methuen introductions to development)
Bibliography: p.
Includes index.
1. Developing countries—Economic conditions.
2. Economic development—Case studies.
I. Title. II. Series.
HC59.7.C59   1987   338.9'009172'4   86-23758

ISBN 0-416-92080-2

Contents

Acknowledgements

The author would like to thank Mr Chris Lewis for drawing the diagrams and maps.

1
Introduction

General introduction

Are you using this book in a school or college in north-west Europe or North America? If so, it is highly probable that your family will live in a home with several rooms, will own a television set, a telephone, and at least one car. You will have running water in the home, will consume more food than is considered necessary to have a healthy body, will have quick access to good health services and will travel away from home yearly for a holiday.

Unless you have spent some time in Third World countries and visited different places within them, you will perhaps imagine that most citizens of such countries simply have a watered-down version of your own existence. In reality in some Third World countries a few 'privileged' families may have material standards comparable to yours but the vast majority do not. As a citizen of a comparatively 'rich' country you may not only want to learn about the Third World but also to do something to help the citizens of poorer countries.

Our economic life is closely tied through trade and other international transactions to all parts of the Third World. It is a matter of self-interest to learn about what is happening there. Our society has long been influenced by Christian ideas, one of which is the need to help the poor. There is also a strong socialist tradition, going back a century or more in Europe, which regards inequality, or excessive inequality, as undesirable, if not evil. Poverty should be removed, not alleviated. Whether one's concern for the less well-off should extend only to the boundary of one's own country or should reach out world-wide is a matter of controversy.

If you are a geographer then you will probably already have learned more than most people about the world. The purpose of this book is to give you some guidelines on how to study the Third World from a geographical perspective. Other books in this series will cover particular topics in greater depth.

In order to introduce various major features and problems of the Third World, a number of ingredients have been distinguished in this book.

1   Human population: everyone a consumer and some also producers.
2   Natural resources: items such as soil, water, minerals and natural vegetation which existed before humans began to organize the world for their own benefit.
3   Means of production: farm buildings and equipment, factories, schools, which produce goods and services.
4   Products: these are broadly of two main kinds, those such as food, clothing, television sets, which people 'consume', and those such as tractors, rails and machine tools, which replace or maintain existing means of production or create new productive capacity.
5   Links between places: necessary for the movement of goods, people and information because production does not all take place in one location.
6   International transactions: needed because the world is divided into some two hundred distinct political units, technically defined as sovereign states (we shall refer to them simply as countries). Each is to some extent a sealed-off and self-sufficient territorial unit of organization. A definitive list of all countries, whatever their size, is given yearly in the *United Nations Statistical Yearbook*.
7   The ideological, cultural and political views and policies of other people: these must be appreciated, even if not accepted, by you or me. They greatly influence the way countries are organized.

Historical perspective

Was there ever a time in the history of human existence in the world when all human communities were identical? That is a difficult question to answer because the evidence is that for the last several thousand years there have always been marked differences. Long before the Industrial Revolution some people such as the aboriginal population of Australia and many communities in the tropical forests of the world lived in the simplest way imaginable. Indeed some still do and, because such people have few wants and unlimited resources, they could be described as affluent. More frequently, however, we think of other parts of the world where fertile agricultural land and cities existed. In such places at least some people lived in considerable luxury. The development gap has been around for quite a long time, a point that is well worth thinking about.

Machines began to be used widely for production and transport more than two hundred years ago. In particular, coal was used to drive the machines in the earlier decades of the Industrial Revolution, first of all in Britain, in the eighteenth century. Those countries that quickly followed the example of Britain, such as France, Germany and the USA, and later Japan, Italy and Russia, among others, came by the middle of the present century to have a huge lead over most other countries in the means to produce large quantities of goods and services.

The technological contrast between Europe (including Russia) plus the United States of America and Japan on the one hand and the rest of the world on the other was made wider because the Americas, much of Asia and almost all of Africa were for varying lengths of time colonies of European powers. From the time when Spain and Portugal acquired their first colonies in Mexico, Peru and Brazil in the sixteenth century until the present century, the general policy of the European powers was to forbid or discourage industrialization in their colonies. Only industries that were needed to supply local needs or to extract and process food (such as sugar) and minerals (such as silver, later copper and many others) were allowed. The British control of India was powerful enough in the last century to force the closure of domestic cotton-textile industries there. Raw cotton grown in India was shipped from India to Lancashire mills, and some of the cloth and clothing was exported back to India.

The idea that the colonies or ex-colonies of Europe, most of them in warmer latitudes than Europe itself, should serve as a source of food, beverages, spices and raw materials for the industrial countries, lasted until after the Second World War (1939–45). In the late 1940s the British government, Labour at the time, supported a costly and disastrous scheme to grow groundnuts in East Africa, particularly in Tanganyika (now Tanzania), for export to Britain. Highland areas in neighbouring Kenya were still seen as a potential area of settlement for 'white' settlers. At great cost militarily the French government tried to support several hundred thousand French settlers in Algeria in the 1950s against growing opposition from the Algerians. The colonial period was nearly over, however, because of a new development of world importance.

During the Second World War, shortly before the defeat of Germany and Japan in 1945, the leaders of the existing countries of the time were getting together to work out a new and, they hoped, a better world. The result was the formation of the United Nations Organization. Like its predecessor, the League of Nations, the United Nations had a primary aim: to maintain peace in the world. For forty years there has indeed been no world war, but there have been many local and regional conflicts.

A second aim of the United Nations was to hasten the removal of colonial rule from the remaining colonies of the world. By the early 1960s, almost all the former colonies of West European powers had become new independent states. In contrast, the many non-Russian colonies of the Russian Empire remained within the Soviet Union after the takeover by the Communist Party from its tsarist predecessor.

A third aim of the United Nations and its various associated institutions has been to assist the poorer countries of the world. In this respect, the United Kingdom and France, having accepted the loss of their colonies, have, through the British Commonwealth and the French Community, continued to trade extensively with many former colonies and to provide them with assistance of various kinds. All the richer countries send assistance to the poorer ones, through both state and private channels. Some contributors are more generous than others and some put more conditions on the use of the aid than others.

Although a number of former colonies, mainly small ones, have become independent since the early 1960s the world political map has remained fairly stable since then. However, several different groupings of countries have now been recognized. When one talks about the developing world or the Third World, therefore, it is important to make it clear which sets of countries come under which heading. In the next section various terms will be discussed.

Terms and definitions related to development

How you refer to something does not necessarily affect or change it, but in order that we should be clear about terms used with regard to development a number must be examined and if possible defined.

1   Rich and poor countries. On the basis of gross national product (see below) per inhabitant (in us dollars), Switzerland ($16,400) and Kuwait ($18,200) must qualify as rich, regardless of how unevenly the dollar equivalents are distributed among the population, since the world average is only $2760. Bangladesh with $130 and Ethiopia with $140 per inhabitant must be poor. It is very difficult, however, to draw a line somewhere near the middle of the range of countries.

2   'North and South' is a fashionable classification but is also rather vague. When reference is made to North and South hemispheres, the geographical split is absurd, because most of the population of the poor countries lives in the northern hemisphere (which includes both India and China). What is more, some prosperous countries, including Australia, New Zealand, Argentina and Uruguay, are actually located to the south of 'The South'.

3   Another common classification of countries is into industrialized (or modernized) and non-industrialized countries. Strictly speaking, every country in the world except the very smallest has some industry. The

term here implies that industry makes a major contribution to total production of goods and services in an industrialized country. At the same time various sectors of production would be quite highly mechanized, consumption of energy would be high and each worker in agriculture would be producing enough to support several or many other people.

4 The term 'Third World' has been in use for many years now. Although easy to remember, Third World is unfortunate because there is confusion over what is meant by Third. The original First and Second Worlds were based on political or ideological aspects. The western democracies (as they call themselves) were the First World and the Eastern socialist countries (as they are described by the Soviet Union) are the Second World. The Third World consisted of 'neutral' countries (in a political sense) including among others Yugoslavia, Egypt and India. So there has been a transfer of meaning because Third World now popularly implies the poorer countries.

5 Perhaps the most appropriate terms for us to use are developed and developing, though not everyone agrees exactly what development implies, and some even doubt whether development is desirable anyway. Most, but not all, developed countries are highly industrialized and generally have a high productivity per person employed. Income per inhabitant is also used to classify countries according to level of development.

The term development is used by the United Nations which categorizes the countries of the world into the following groups (*Statistical Yearbook*, 1979/80, p. 422):

1 Developed Market Economies: Europe apart from the Centrally Planned Economies, plus the United States of America, Canada, Australia, New Zealand, Japan, Israel, South Africa.

2 Centrally Planned Economies: the Soviet Union and its partners in East Europe (but not Yugoslavia) plus China, Mongolia, the Korean Democratic People's Republic and Vietnam in Asia.

3 Developing Market Economies, including Cuba, which should really be included under 2.

Although it is not stated explicitly in the *Yearbook*, the countries under 2 form developed and developing subsets, the European group being developed, the Asian group developing. In Soviet foreign trade publications (*Vneshnyaya torgovlya SSSR*) all the countries in group 2 are referred to as socialist.

A thought-provoking additional note about the grouping of countries comes with the United Nations *Statistical Yearbook*, 1981, table 179, in

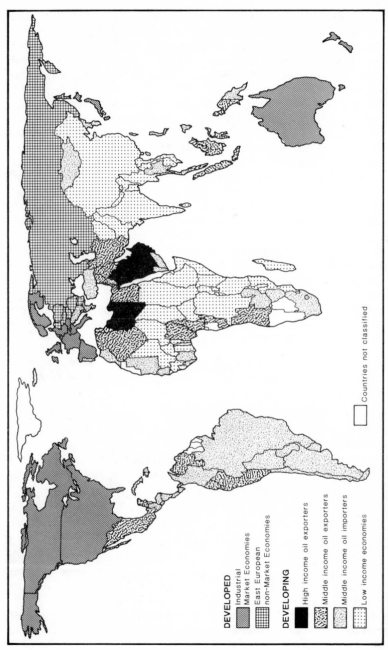

Figure 1.1 Countries of the world grouped according to type of economy. Low-income economies less than $400 per inhabitant in 1983. Countries with fewer than 1 million inhabitants are not shaded. Projection: Peter's equal area.
Source: World Development Report (1985), pp. 170–1.

DEVELOPED
Industrial
Market Economies

East European
non-Market Economies

DEVELOPING
High income oil exporters

Middle income oil exporters

Middle income oil importers

Low income economies

Countries not classified

which the grouping of countries into developed and developing for trade statistics is given: 'This classification is intended for statistical convenience and does not, necessarily, express a judgement about the stage reached by a particular country in the development process'. 'Stage' and gross national product per inhabitant do not correlate perfectly. In the classification already quoted above from the 1979/80 *Yearbook* there are many developing countries with a higher gross national product per inhabitant than Portugal, which is defined as 'developed'. The diplomatic quotation from the 1981 *Yearbook* is also of interest because it assumes that there *is* 'a development process' and that there *are* 'stages' in the process. This assumption has been questioned by some as simplistic or even unrealistic.

Other international bodies divide the world up differently. For example the World Bank and various other institutions divide the countries of the world into developed and developing for their own purposes. How do they do this? In the *World Development Report 1985* of the influential World Bank, countries are grouped both by income and by region. Gross domestic product and gross national product are two measures that are slightly different. Both are widely used. Gross domestic product (GDP) is defined (pp. x–xi of the *Report*) as 'the total final output of goods and services produced by an economy – that is, by residents and non-residents'. Gross national product (GNP) differs in counting only that output produced by residents, but adds income from abroad. So a money value can be used to put a quantity to everything produced in a country in, say, a year. Unfortunately the Centrally Planned countries (self-defined as 'socialist') do not officially make a comparable calculation, though this can be estimated.

The World Bank uses gross national product to distinguish low-income developing economies, those in 1983 with a GNP per person of less than US $400 per person and middle-income developing countries with US $400 or more per person. Industrial (therefore developed) market economies are members of the Organization of Economic Co-operation and Development, apart from Greece, Portugal and Turkey, which are classed as middle-income developing countries.

Formerly countries were grouped in some publications as developed and underdeveloped. The term 'underdeveloped' was regarded as disparaging, while 'developing' sounds more respectable and seems to hold out the expectation or hope that positive change will take place. The term 'less developed' has also been used and you may meet the initials LDC, short for Less Developed Countries. In addition, occasionally, the terms 'undeveloped' and 'overdeveloped' are used. One might perhaps refer to the Amazon region of South America as undeveloped and the older industrial regions of Europe, with exhausted coalfields and declining industries, as overdeveloped. It could be useful to have a discussion and consider how the various terms can best be used in your studies.

Statistics and snags

So far reference has only been made to gross national product as a way of comparing countries and determining for organizational purposes which countries shall be referred to as developing. We must now look more carefully both at money and at other measures and note some problems and drawbacks in their definition and use.

It is important at the start of a series of books on Third World Development to examine the term gross national product (GNP). The use of money units to assess development gives rise to problems. The real value of the unit of currency of each country is likely to change appreciably over short periods of time, usually dropping in value with inflation. To complicate the situation, for international comparisons that everyone can understand it is helpful to use a single currency, not the currency of each country. It is common to convert other currencies to the US dollar at exchange rates of the time. But the rate can change very quickly.

There is a case for looking at different products in relation to one another instead of just juggling with large quantities of money units, though things can get complicated. President Nyerere of Tanzania is quoted as complaining some years ago that in the late 1960s you only needed to export 17 tonnes of sisal to pay for a Fordson tractor, whereas by the mid-1970s you needed 22 tonnes.* In the early 1970s I could have bought one of the new microcomputers for £2000, while for the same money I could have bought about 8000 gallons of petrol for my car. Now I can get a better microcomputer for £400 but only 200 gallons of petrol for that money. What a difference!

In making comparisons between countries it may be helpful at times to use other units of measurement instead of money, though this means taking into consideration only part at a time of the total production or consumption of goods and services. A useful product to measure is energy (fuel and power), which can be calculated in thermal units, or in terms of coal equivalent (for example one tonne of oil is equivalent roughly to 1.5 tonnes of coal). You might feel safe here because a tonne of coal is always a tonne of coal. Over the last two centuries or so, however, the amount of energy derived from a given weight of coal has increased enormously through efficiency of use. A snag, but never mind.

When at last you have decided on some suitable sets of numerical data to illustrate points about Third World Development, you may find the numbers so large that they do not mean anything to you, or so complicated in definition that their significance is lost. Never trust a set of numbers. I shall just quote two errors that I found in the United Nations *Statistical*

* Tonne is the spelling now widely used for a metric ton, which is 1000 kilograms.

Yearbook, 1979/80: on p. 844 Senegal is credited with 10 'population per physician'. Nearby Mali has nearly 25,000 population per physician, while England and Wales has 630, so something must be wrong. In the same book on p. 365, Zaire is recorded as having assembled 2,100,000 motor vehicles in 1975, and nearly as many each year for several years before that. Zaire only had about 30 million people and very few roads and motor vehicles, so it seems an awfully large number.

Whether or not you like numbers, large or small, accurate or estimated, you have to use some, and tables 1.1–1.6 contain some introductory sets of data. The countries in each table have been selected to provide representatives from different levels on each numerical scale and from each major region of the world. The purpose of the six tables that follow is to draw your attention to the very big differences between countries. The first two sets, area and population, are comparisons of total size. The other four show values per inhabitant, eliminating the direct effect of differences in size. Before you read further, look at each table in turn and note down your first impressions: are you surprised at the values or are they roughly as you expected?

A major problem in the interpretation of numerical data arises from the need to add or aggregate data and use averages and other statistical measures. There are so many people, tonnes of rice, telephones and tonne-kilometres of goods transported about the place that data have to be aggregated into classes (e.g. people into age groups, income groups or types of economic occupation) or into convenient regions (e.g. states in Brazil or provinces in China, countries of the world). Sometimes very large spreads of values are concealed in averages. Some examples will illustrate the snags.

Table 1.1 Surface area of selected countries in square kilometres

The six largest		Six selected small		Six others	
USSR	22,402,200	Luxembourg	2,590	South Africa	1,221,040
Canada	9,976,140	Hong Kong	1,050	France	547,030
China	9,596,960	Bahrain	622	UK	244,050
USA	9,363,120	Antigua	442	Bangladesh	144,000
Brazil	8,511,970	Seychelles	280	Haiti	27,750
Australia	7,686,850	Monaco	1	Kuwait	17,820

Source: United Nations, *Statistical Yearbook* (1979/80).

Points for consideration:
1 How accurate is the measure of area?
2 Are water surfaces included?
3 Is total land area a realistic measure of productive land and the availability of minerals?

Table 1.2 Total population of selected countries, 1985

The six largest		Six selected small		Six others	
China	1,042,000,000	Gabon	1,000,000	Mexico	79,700,000
India	762,200,000	Cyprus	621,000	UK	56,400,000
USSR	278,000,000	Qatar	210,000	Ethiopia	36,000,000[2]
USA	238,900,000	Seychelles	63,000	Sri Lanka	16,400,000
Indonesia	168,400,000	Bermuda	59,000	Saudi Arabia	11,200,000
Brazil	138,400,000	Tristan da Cunha	186[1]	Tunisia	7,200,000

Notes: [1] 1938 census
[2] no census ever held
Source: Population Reference Bureau, *World Population Data Sheet* (1985).

Points for consideration:
1 Does total population equal power and influence in the world?
2 If countries differ so much in total population size, why do individual states have only one representative in the United National General Assembly (the Soviet Union has three)?

Table 1.3 Consumption of commercial sources of energy in kilograms of coal-equivalent per inhabitant in 1982

Selected developed countries		Selected developing countries	
USA	9,430	Honduras	240
Australia	7,160	Indonesia	230
USSR	5,770	India	200
UK	4,540	Bangladesh	50
Japan	3,500	Ethiopia	30
Spain	2,280	Nepal	10

Source: United Nations, *Energy Statistics Yearbook* (1982).

Points for consideration:
1 How is it that an American can consume nearly a thousand times as much energy as a Nepalese?
2 Do some countries need more fuel for heating than others?
3 How do the very low consumers top up their minute consumption levels?
4 How much does private motoring use up?
5 If the developed countries used less energy, could the developing countries have more?

Table 1.4   People per physician, mostly in 1980 or late 1970s

Favourable		Unfavourable	
Israel	370	Haiti	10,000
USA	520	Bangladesh	11,000
Uruguay	580	Afghanistan	20,000
France	580	Niger	34,000
England and Wales	650	Burundi	45,000
Cuba, Libya	700	Burkina Faso*	54,000
Japan, Kuwait	780	Ethiopia	58,000

Note: * formerly Upper Volta
Source: United Nations, *Statistical Yearbook* (1981).

Points for consideration:
1   Note that a high score here means 'unfavourable'.
2   Are more doctors needed in relation to population in some areas than in others?
3   What other ways can you think of to measure the level of health-care facilities in a region?

Table 1.5   The number of scientists and engineers engaged in research and experimental development per million total population, early 1980s

Japan	3,480	Brazil	180
USA	2,670	Mexico	80
German FR	1,820	Philippines	70
UK	1,390	India	40
Italy	670	Nigeria	20
Egypt	230	Bangladesh	20

Source: United Nations, *Statistical Yearbook* (1981).

Points for consideration:
1   What an enormous gap here! Actually the Soviet Union claims to have over 1.5 million, or about 5,600 per million people, but the definition may be rather elastic.
2   Surely the less developed countries should be the ones that need more researchers, not far, far fewer? Watch Japan.

Table 1.6   Gross national product in US dollars per inhabitant, early to mid 1980s

Very high		Selected intermediate		Very low	
Kuwait	18,180	UK	9,050	Malawi	210
Switzerland	16,390	Spain	4,800	Burma	180
USA	14,090	Venezuela	4,100	Nepal	170
Saudi Arabia	12,180	Mexico	2,240	Mali	150
German FR	11,420	Portugal	2,190	Ethiopia	140
Australia	10,780	Korean Republic	2,010	Bangladesh	130

Source: Population Reference Bureau, *World Population Data Sheet* (1985).

Points for consideration
1   GNP is important because it covers all goods and services produced.
2   It is a simple, shorthand indicator of the total 'cake' and the average 'slice' each citizen would get.
3   It is unsatisfactory because it is measured in money units (drawbacks discussed in the text) and does not measure happiness (but what does?).
4   It is really a measure of the rate at which non-renewable natural resources are being used up.

In India the average life expectancy is 53 years. However, about 12 per cent of all deaths take place among infants before they reach their first birthday and quite a lot more among young children. Very few Indians die in their fifties, many living on well beyond that age. In China in 1981 there were on average about 450 people per telephone, but in the cities the number was only 100 (still large) and in rural areas over 1000 (no wonder telephones are used communally). A recent healthcare figure for Ethiopia (see table 1.4) is 58,000 people to each physician, yet the availability must be well above this in the capital Addis Ababa, while I have one earlier figure for a province in Ethiopia that had two doctors for 800,000 people.

With a large data set it may be difficult to discover from the columns or rows of numbers if there is anything of particular interest, in which case it may be helpful to show the data graphically. In figure 1.2 the twenty largest countries of the world in population in 1985 are plotted in order of GNP per inhabitant. The graph would be more realistic if each bar had a width (vertically) proportional to its population, but it does bring out a gap between developed (Soviet Union and Italy) and developing (Mexico) and people do like to see things falling just into two classes (a dichotomy). Further down the list of countries ranked by population size in table 1.6 there are some countries with GNPs in US$ per inhabitant between the Soviet Union at 6350 and Mexico at 2240; for example, Israel 5360, Bulgaria 4400, Venezuela 4100, Yugoslavia 2570, but far more below 2000.

At this point it is worth noting a less obvious feature of the graph.

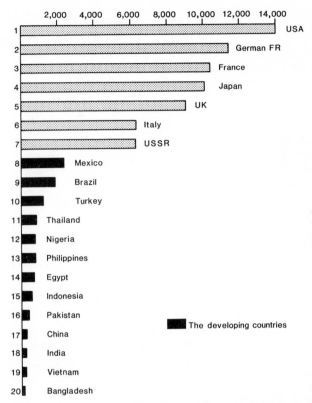

Figure 1.2   The twenty largest countries of the world in population ranked in order of gross national product per inhabitant in the 1980s.

Relatively, the Italian GNP is nearly three times as high as the Mexican, while the United States GNP is little more than twice as high as the Italian. On the other hand the absolute dollar gap per inhabitant between Mexico and Italy is only $4000, while that between Italy and the United States is more than $7500. Always consider this comparison between relative and absolute difference. You could argue here that a gap of about $1000 (or however much) between France and the German Federal Republic does not mean so much as a gap of the same amount between Bangladesh and Turkey.

What conditions do the numerical data represent on the ground?

One could go on for a long time noting all the problems in the use of numerical data, even before moving on to complicated quantitative methods for processing large data sets. As geographers we should also be finding out what real people and places are like. Thankfully photographic and verbal accounts can help one to see what conditions are like 'on the ground'. Even though the average citizen of Bangladesh is credited with US$130 a year, films made in the country, usually of disasters, show that they seem to have clothes. I remember noting in Ethiopia in 1973, however, that many of the village people there wore only rags, rather like odd pieces of sack sewn together. A child in a place called Lalibela gladly accepted one of my vests and immediately put it on under his jersey. I later sent some parcels of old clothes, but the children I met in Lalibela may now have died of hunger.

Case study A

Housing in Haiti

What are conditions really like in the very poor countries? Probably the first comprehensive account of conditions in a very poor country produced by the United Nations was *A Mission to Haiti*, published in 1949. The report includes a description I remember vividly, quoting an expert who wrote about rural housing in 1948 (p. 38):

> The family has limited resources with which to rent a home, let alone buy a house. Consequently, it has been the tradition over more than 100 years for most Haitians of low income to build their own homes. The typical house consists of a single room, usually with less than 100 square feet, bare dirt floor, wood frame construction, woven clay mixed with grass (not unlike the adobe walls found in the south-western United States and Mexico) and a thatched roof. The homes have no sanitary facilities or running water. The cooking is done on the ground outside, over a metal brazier and charcoal fire. A handmade bed, chair, chest, counter and metal eating utensils are all one usually finds inside. The more fortunate families have a community privy nearby. The land is frequently rented from a large land owner. Sometimes a plot of ground is handed down from father to son and is owned outright and sometimes the dwelling or shack is built on public property. Thousands upon thousands of Haitian

Case study A (*continued*)

families in urban as well as rural areas live in this fashion. Generations have lived in this same way.

My impression after my first visit to Haiti in 1985, a brief one, was that housing conditions have not changed much in Haiti since 1948. There are, however, about twice as many people living there now as there were then.

In another part of the same report there is a commentary on health conditions in the rural areas of Haiti. Note that about 90 per cent of the population was rural then (p. 61):

Lacking as a rule the very essentials of wholesome housing, the peasant huts, described in a previous section, are difficult to keep reasonably sanitary. Rarely has a peasant family more than one bed, if any, and several people share it simultaneously; the less fortunate sleep on mats on the bare ground. The water available for use in the household seldom fulfils the demands of hygiene; as properly capped wells are scarce, the rural population commonly relies on more or less polluted surface water for drinking and cooking, washing and bathing. Latrines and other toilet facilities are mostly lacking. In the circumstances, obviously, a heavy task confronts the Haitian health authorities, whose work in the rugged countryside is further complicated by the very poor state of communications, causing whole areas to be practically isolated during the major part of the rainy season.

In the early 1980s the GNP per inhabitant in Haiti (see case study A, pp. 14–5) was some US$320. This is the lowest in the whole of Latin America and is due to heavy dependence on agriculture, together with enormous pressure of population on very limited land resources. To some extent this is a delayed effect of the policy of the French government in the eighteenth century to concentrate large numbers of slaves from Africa in its main colony in the tropics. The population of Haiti is only about 6 million but in numerous demographically small countries in eastern and middle Africa about 250 million people in all also have an average of about US$300 per head, while over 1000 million in South Asia have about US$250 per head and, depending on how the GNP of China is assessed, another 1000 million or more people here have somewhere between US$300 and US$500 per head.

In my own travels elsewhere in Latin America I have seen conditions similar to those described in Haiti. I remember clearly a brief visit to a village called Chaquicocha in the Central Andes of Peru in 1970. Several hundred people made a living from several hundred hectares of land. From the crops and livestock they raised they had to feed themselves and provide a surplus, largely of animal products, to sell outside the village. They had to buy tools, fuel, building materials, such as metal sheeting and glass, basic necessities such as salt, and 'luxury' items such as sugar, beer and school books elsewhere in Peru. There were no health care facilities in the village and only a primary school. Population was kept at a minimum level through illnesses causing the death of many young children, and through migration away to the cities, often of the more ambitious and enterprising young people.

Numerical data for developing countries generally show that people in the cities have much higher living standards on average than those in the countryside. In reality, many urban dwellers live in very poor conditions. Many live in slums, for which they pay low rents. Others live in self-built squatter settlements (or shanty towns) on land not in use at a particular time (empty lots) or unlikely to be used anyway (steep hillsides, river beds, desert land outside the city).

My first encounter with a squatter settlement was in Lima, Peru (see plates 1.1 and 1.2), where I helped to make a survey of a newly created *barriada*, called Ciudad de Dios (city of God), which had been 'built' in one night by some 20,000 squatters. A few weeks later many had left but thousands were still living there. At first their homes were mostly made of walls of cane matting, with the floor of sand and no roof. I remember visiting one dwelling where a couple with a baby were living. They slept on mats on the sandy floor and the only possessions they had were a wooden box and an enamel bowl. The local government was not providing anything but water delivered in an old tanker lorry.

Such shanty towns gradually become organized and improved but they are still very squalid and many are inconveniently located a long way from where people work. In 1955 we estimated that there were about 100,000 people already living in the shanty towns of Lima, about one person in twelve. In 1985 there were more than a million living in shanty towns out of Lima's total population of 5 million. You can see far out along the road to the north new shanty towns springing up, new *pueblos jóvenes* or 'young settlements'.

The average GNP per inhabitant of a country fails to show huge income differences between different sectors of the population. There are some enormously wealthy families in Latin American countries and also in African and Asian ones. I remember being particularly struck in 1969 in Rio de Janeiro by seeing on the same afternoon, on two separate occasions, a dog on a lead being exercised along the street by a man driving a car, in one

Plates 1.1. and 1.2   Two scenes from Cuidad de Dios (City of God), Lima, Peru, early 1955. *Barriadas* (squatter settlements) built outside Lima in the desert. Since 1955 the number of people living in squatter settlements, more recently referred to officially as *pueblos jóvenes*, has probably increased tenfold.

instance a Mercedes. The very wealthy may have servants not only for the domestic work, cooking and child care, but also for the car and their pets.

In most market economy countries there are also professional workers and some comparatively well-off office and factory workers who live in conditions roughly similar to those familiar to most of us in the developed world. Many are concentrated in clearly defined areas within the larger cities in the developing countries. They have household gadgets and cars, often imported, reasonable health care facilities and a good standard of education for their children. They tend to live rather precariously, as if in outliers of the developed world, surrounded by massive numbers of poor people. Case study B contains part of a letter from a Peruvian friend of British origin, sent to my wife in Nottingham in 1983, a tale of woe to say the least.

Case study B

Floods and inflation in Peru

A letter from Callao, Peru, 10 April 1983 (S/ stands for *sol*, the Peruvian unit of currency; at that time the rate of exchange was about 2000 soles to the pound sterling).

You have probably heard about the flooding in Piura, Tumbes, Trujillo, Lambayeque, where there are thousands homeless and the water in some places is more than a metre high. Also Huaraz, Chimbote, and now Chosica! The rains in Piura are torrential and all the rivers have flooded homes, plantations, etc. In the Central Railway and Carretera Central the landslides were terrific and on one occasion buried a bus full of passengers! The road is destroyed in many parts and it will take the Railway about 4 months and millions of dollars to repair the damage. It is heart-breaking to see the views on TV. Due to these landslides the Water Co. had to close the locks as the water coming in was full of mud, so, at first, we were taken by surprise and were about 2 days without a drop of water! After that we would be given water for about an hour, but only a dribble which did not reach any tap but that of the bath, and we had to quickly fill up all we could. And all this when temperature was fluctuating between 86 °F and 90 °F, when everyone required a bath! These last two days we have more water, but it is cut off at 1 p.m. and sometimes does not come until the next day.

Case study B (*continued*)

Next comes sugar. Do you know we have been without sugar for over two months? I said it was the 'Mil y Una Noche' tale, because every time the Minister spoke he gave a different reason. The truth is that it was all exported and no reserve was made for internal consumption. Now we have received sugar from Bolivia and Chile, but it is still not available to the general public. There is a lot of speculation, and some people have paid over S/2000 for a kilo! But I don't know how they get it. The 'official' price is S/445 for white and S/360 rubia. At home all have condensed milk (now S/1110 a tin), but I have my coffee without, and buy chancaca to eat alone.

Now, with the excuse of the 'huaicos' prices in the market went haywire. The Government has *tried* to control this, but that is as far as they have got. Potatoes are S/700 and S/800 kilo, lettuce *one* S/1000, celery S/2000, tomatoes S/800, beans S/1500 K [kg], quinua S/1000 K and lemons *2 for S/500*. Yet, authorities have found cases of lemons that were hidden and have rotted.

Next Banco Comercial (Bancoper). This has been a terrific blow, but it has been closed as they had speculated with their capital. The Banco Continental has taken over their obligations and it has been guaranteed that all clients will recover their money. But what will happen to the hundreds of employees we don't know. I have several friends who have accounts with Bancoper. It is such a disgrace and scandal. This is the second bank that has been closed down. The previous one was BIC (Banco Industrial de la Construcción).

To raise funds to rebuild all those departments that have been flooded and destroyed, the Government is planning to issue special bonds to be put up for sale, but all workers earning from S/300,000 monthly will be paid 10% of their remuneration in bonds for one year! People are not pleased with this, but really it is a necessity.

We have to present a new Auto-Avalio to our property this month, and the Municipalities, too, went hay-wire over prices. Our land was quoted at S/45,000 sq m, when in 1980 it was S/5,000! Also prices given for construction were terrific. The Government had to intervene and obliged them to quote more reasonable prices. Now our land is S/20,000 sq m which is more reasonable. Our property has risen from S/3,045,228 in 1980 to S/14,468,981 after deducting 47% depreciation as it is 50 years old! We are as bad as the 'country' 'mendigos sentados en un trono de oro'! [A beggar sitting on a golden throne.]

Key ideas

1   The Third World is linked to us through trade and other international transactions.
2   The development gap has existed for many hundreds of years.
3   It has traditionally been thought that the colonies (or ex-colonies) of Europe should provide resources for the industrial countries.
4   Considerable problems exist in defining 'development' and a number of interpretations are placed on the term.
5   Although gross national product per capita is usually used to compare the levels of development of different countries, this indicator does present a number of problems of interpretation.
6   A large number of indicators can be used to measure 'development'.

2
Natural resources

Introduction

In chapter 1 it was proposed that natural resources should be classed as a distinct ingredient for development. Everyone who studies development knows more or less what the term 'natural resources' includes. On the whole, however, development studies in the last few decades have understandably given more importance to levels of application of technology and to industrialization than to availability of natural resources.

It has long been appreciated that people in some parts of the world are better endowed than others with natural resources (table 2.1). In some countries, such as Japan, Switzerland, Singapore and Hong Kong, high levels of industrialization and high living standards have been achieved on the basis of relatively few natural resources. As already stressed, technology differentiates rich and poor more than natural resources do. However if all or most parts of the world achieved the high level of industrialization of Japan, for example, then resource-rich countries like Australia and Canada, and regions like Siberia (Soviet Union) and Amazonia (shared by several South American countries) would be the ones at an advantage.

For the purposes of this book the term natural resource refers to anything in the natural world that is not the work of humans. For simplicity natural resources can be subdivided into two main kinds: bioclimatic and mineral. These terms must be defined.

1   Bioclimatic resources consist of the soil or water bodies in which plants grow, plus heat needed for their growth, and the water also needed for

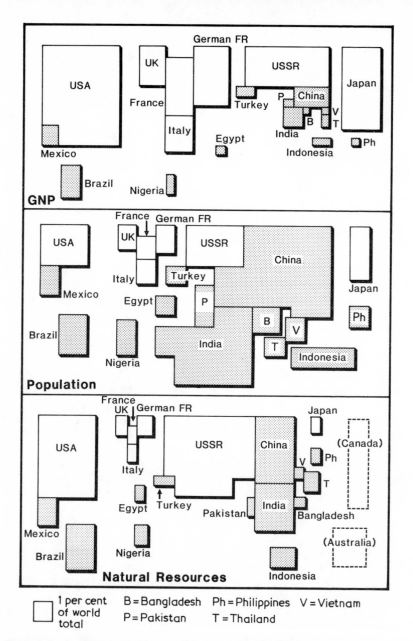

Figure 2.1 A comparison of the twenty largest countries of the world in population with regard to absolute size of gross national product, population and natural resources. Third World countries are shaded. Canada and Australia have been added to the original twenty countries in the Natural Resources section.

plants on land. The products are plant or animal, though the ingredients for their growth are, of course, mineral.

2   Mineral resources are of two main kinds, fossil fuels (coal, lignite, oil and natural gas) and non-fuel minerals. Non-fuel minerals are usually subdivided into metallic and non-metallic.

Some natural resources, such as direct solar energy and hydroelectric power, do not easily fall into the two main categories. Air may be thought of as a natural resource, but it is largely taken for granted because it is universally available.

Natural resources are fixed in location or, like water and air, flow in cycles. The *products* from natural resources, such as cereals from the land or copper ore extracted from a mine, can be moved from place to place. In contrast, natural resources themselves are fixed in location so it is meaningful to estimate how many natural resources different countries and regions have. Some natural resources, such as the fishing grounds at some distance from the coasts and minerals on the ocean bed, are in what is often referred to as 'the commons'.

Some natural resources are regarded as exhaustible or non-renewable while others are not exhaustible. Once you have burned a supply of coal or oil it has literally gone up in smoke or fumes. If you make steel from iron ore the deposit is depleted, although the steel can sometimes be recycled later as scrap. If you grow a crop of rice or wheat in a field only a little material is removed from the total soil.

In reality, some non-renewable natural resources are gradually accumulating, though for example it took many millions of years for the oil used in the last hundred years to be formed. At the same time there is a danger in taking soil for granted and assuming that it cannot be exhausted or lost in some other way. The increased mechanization of agriculture and changing farming practices have indeed led to devastating soil erosion in many parts of the world this century. Some good agricultural land is lost through the building of cities, roads and other construction works.

Bioclimatic resources

The Food and Agriculture Organization (FAO) of the United Nations gathers data about land use, the production of crops and the raising of livestock in the whole world. Such a task is difficult because data have to be obtained from about two hundred countries, large and small. In developing countries, in particular, the gathering of information about agriculture is difficult and many of the data published by FAO are just intelligent estimates.

In the inventory of different types of land use published by the FAO for each country four categories are used: arable (plus permanent crops such as

Plates 2.1 and 2.2 Two scenes from China, near Guilin (1980) and outside Nanjing (1982). Rugged conditions in some regions of China, arid conditions in other regions, confine the cultivated areas to 10 per cent of the total national territory. Simple methods of cultivation are still widely practised. Night soil 'donated' by the residents of the village in special toilets helps to boost yields.

coffee and fruit trees), permanent pasture, forest and woodland, and other (including both urban land and waste such as desert). Of the total land area of the world of 13,077 million hectares (ha) (or nearly 131 million km^2), a little over 11 per cent is arable, 24 per cent natural pasture and 31 per cent forest. The remaining third is waste or built on.

The bioclimatic resources of the countries of the world have been grouped into fourteen regions in table 2.1 and the areas of the three types of used land are shown, together with total land area and population for each region. Arable land is the type of most importance since in general yields of food and of raw materials per unit of area are much greater than those from pasture or forest.

Table 2.1 The land resources of fourteen major world regions (population in millions, area in millions of hectares)

	Region	Population	Land area	Arable[1]	Permanent pasture	Forest
1	Australia and New Zealand	18	789	47	459	116
2	Canada	25	922	46	24	326
3	USA	232	913	191	238	284
4	USSR and MPR	272	2,384	234	496	935
5	East Europe	130	126	54	21	38
6	West Europe	352	347	87	64	117
7	Japan	118	37	5	1	25
8	Central America	130	301	37	94	71
9	South America	252	1,753	139	455	933
10	Africa south of Sahara	383	2,155	145	663	632
11	North Africa and South-west Asia	292	1,490	104	320	107
12	South Asia	912	395	202	18	75
13	South-east Asia	456	475	81	22	266
14	China	1,021	933	101	286	128
	All developed[2]	1,186	5,485	675	1,261	1,832
	All developing	3,407	7,592	979	1,901	2,258
	World	4,593	13,077	1,473	3,162	4,090

Notes: [1] Includes fallow and permanent crops.
 [2] Regions 1–7 plus South Africa and Israel from regions 10 and 11 respectively.
Source: Food and Agriculture Organization, *Production Yearbook* (1983), vol. 37, tables 1, 3.

Throughout the last two hundred years or so there has been a gradual increase in the arable area of the world. In the last forty years, however, the population of the world has almost doubled but the area of arable land has only increased by about 10 per cent. Most of the increase in food production required to support the growing population has been obtained through higher yields, particularly in developed countries.

Table 2.2 shows the changing ratio of arable land to inhabitants in some major developing countries over fifty years. Study the data and plot some of the trends on a graph. What do you feel may happen after the year 2000?

It is a matter of controversy as to how much of the present pasture, forest and other land could eventually be used for cultivation. Unless cultivation is extended beyond the present arable areas of the world to match population growth, the amount of land per person will continue to decrease.

The fact that the total arable area of the world has not increased much in recent decades is one major matter of concern. Indeed in some areas arable land has been lost through removal of soil or urbanization (see case study C, p. 27). Another major problem is the very uneven distribution of arable land in relation to population (see table 2.2). Even when allowance is made for double cropping in some countries and for the greater fertility of soil in some places than others, the contrasts are huge. At one extreme, there are over 300 ha of arable land per 100 inhabitants in Australia. At the other, in Japan and the Republic of Korea, the figure is only 4 or 5 ha, and in Hong Kong virtually none. The great increase of population in developing countries in recent decades has helped to leave many such countries unfavourably placed with regard to availability of arable land.

Table 2.2 Hectares of arable land and permanent crops per 100 people

	1951	1963	1974–6	1982	2000*
Mexico	69	62	39	32	29
Brazil	37	40	56	58	48
Colombia	22	30	23	21	17
Nigeria	66	48	46	37	23
Ethiopia	66	55	48	43	27
Morocco	86	56	45	39	24
Egypt	12	9	8	6	4
Turkey	89	85	63	52	42
Iran	101	92	50	34	22
Pakistan	47	36	26	22	15
India	38	35	27	24	18
Bangladesh	19	16	12	10	6
Indonesia	14	17	14	13	11
Philippines	22	23	23	23	19
China	17	14	11	10	9

Note: * author's 'intelligent' estimate.
Source: Food and Agriculture Organization, *Production Yearbook*, various numbers.

Case study C

Notes on natural resources

(from L. R. Brown, 'The Worldwide Loss of Cropland', 1978)

The historical expansion of cultivated land has been closely related to the growth in human numbers. In response to population pressures, farmers moved from valley to valley and continent to continent, gradually extending the area under cultivation until, today, one-tenth of the earth's land surface is under the plow. By the mid-twentieth century, most frontiers had disappeared. Up until that time, increases in world food output had come almost entirely from expanding the area farmed. Increases in land productivity were scarcely perceptible within any given generation. (p. 7)

The question of how much the world's cultivated area can be expanded has been hotly debated during the past 15 years. Some studies contend that it can easily be doubled, while others assume that the opportunities for adding new land will largely be offset by losses – leading to little, if any, increase in the base. The principal difference between such widely varying estimates is explainable in economic terms. The more optimistic projections omit economic constraints whereas the less optimistic ones include them. (p. 35)

Cropland deterioration and loss are not new problems. The Tigris–Euphrates Valley, once described as the Fertile Crescent, may have formerly supported more people than it does today. The food-deficit lands of North Africa were once the granary of the Roman Empire. What is new is the scale of cropland loss and soil deterioration, a problem that affects rich and poor countries alike. Natural soil fertility is now declining on an estimated one-fifth of the world's croplands. (p. 5)

During the final quarter of this century, population is projected to increase by 58 per cent; although slightly smaller in percentage terms, the expected addition of 2.3 billion people would be half again as large as the 1.5 billion added during the third quarter. As the final quarter of this century began, cropland was being lost to nonfarm purposes at a record rate. The abandonment of agricultural land because of severe soil erosion, degradation, and desertification was at an all-time high. The potential for substantial net additions to the world's cropland base was not good. (p. 33)

From the data given in tables 2.3–2.5 we need to consider the following questions. First, in which regions and countries would you expect there to be areas in which the arable area could be extended, and second, how do the countries with little arable land to population feed their populations?

There are a number of ways in which agricultural yields can be increased on existing arable land.

1 Double cropping. In the tropics it is warm enough and wet enough for two crops or even three to be grown on the same piece of land in a year. China has about 100 million ha of arable land but harvests about 150 million ha of crops a year. More pressure is of course put on the nutrients in the soil.

2 Irrigation is essential for cultivation in some areas, such as the famous delta of the Nile in Egypt and in many drier parts of southern Asia and Latin America. Rain supplies may be stored and used later. The area of irrigated land in some developing countries is shown in table 2.4. Why do the percentages of irrigated land to total arable vary so much?

3 Mostly in developed countries in cooler latitudes, greenhouses and hothouses are used to enhance the sun's heat.

4 The use of fertilizers, both animal and chemical, has become widespread in developing countries as well as developed ones. In table 2.5 you will find the average number of kilograms of fertilizer applied in different countries. Look at the contrast between Japan and the United Kingdom with around 400 kg and Argentina and Ethiopia with only 3 kg. Think of reasons for the differences.

Table 2.3 Arable area in hectares per 100 inhabitants

	1951–5	1961–5	1971–5	1985	2000
USA	117	95	95	86	84
Canada, Australia	172	166	158	129	94
Western Europe	33	30	26	24	22
Japan	6	6	5	5	4
USSR	116	102	93	83	73
Latin America	56	51	47	38	28
Africa south of Sahara	72	73	62	49	32
South Asia	38	32	26	19	13
China	16	14	12	10	8
Industrialized market economy	61	56	55	50	46
Less developed	45	40	35	27	19
World	48	44	39	32	25

Note: Eastern Europe, North Africa and the Middle East, South-east and East Asia have been excluded.
Source: Food and Agriculture Organization, *Production Yearbook* (various numbers).

Table 2.4 Irrigated land in selected developing countries

	1974–6 (million ha)	1982 (million ha)	Arable (million ha)	Percentage irrigated
Mexico	4.5	5.2	24	22
Brazil	1.3	2.0	75	3
Ethiopia	2.8	2.5	14	18
Egypt	2.8	2.5	2.5	100
Iran	5.9	4.0	14	29
Pakistan	13.6	14.7	20	74
India	33.6	40.6	170	24
Bangladesh	1.4	1.8	9	20
Indonesia	4.9	5.5	20	28
Philippines	1.1	1.4	12	12
China	42.7	44.8	101	44
World total	187.7	213.4		

Source: Food and Agriculture Organization, *Production Yearbook* (1983).

Table 2.5 Hectares of arable land per 100 inhabitants and fertilizer consumption in kilograms per hectare of arable land in the early 1980s

	Ha of arable land	Fertilizer consumption
Australia	314	24
Canada	187	44
Argentina	129	3
Brazil	58	37
Ethiopia	43	3
Nigeria	37	7
Iran	34	66
Mexico	32	78
India	24	35
Indonesia	13	75
UK	12	365
China	10	158
Bangladesh	10	51
Egypt	6	335
Korean Republic	5	282
Japan	5	412
World	32	

Sources: Food and Agriculture Organization, *Production Yearbook* (1983); World Bank, *World Development Report* (1985).

Energy resources

Most of the energy consumed in the world is provided at present by coal, lignite, oil and natural gas. These fuels are called fossil fuels because they have been formed, mostly long ago, from living matter and are now in mineral form. In the early 1980s coal and lignite provided about 30 per cent of all commercial energy used in the world, oil about 45 per cent and natural gas about 20 per cent. The other main sources included hydro-electric and nuclear power.

The consumption of commercial energy per inhabitant is generally much lower in developing countries than in developed ones, as shown already in chapter 1. On the other hand, non-commercial or local sources of energy are relatively much more important in developing countries. These include human energy, the use of work animals in agriculture and transport, and of fuelwood for cooking and heating.

To appreciate the energy gap we must first examine the way fossil fuel reserves are distributed throughout the world. Its coal and lignite reserves are difficult to measure. Estimates have been made of the recoverable reserves of coal and lignite for a United Nations publication on energy and the countries with the largest coal reserves are given in table 2.6. A few developed countries have between them about two-thirds of the world's recoverable coal reserves. Very few developing countries have any coal at all. Almost all of the lignite in the world is in developed countries. There is plenty of coal in the world, enough already known to exist to last about two hundred years at present rates of extraction and much longer if the 'possible' reserves are considered. From the point of view of the developing countries it is in the wrong places.

The distribution of proven oil reserves is very different from that of coal reserves. The developed countries have less than 20 per cent of all proven

Table 2.6 Estimates of recoverable coal reserves in thousands of millions of tonnes c. 1980

Developed countries		Developing countries	
USA	125	China	99
USSR	109	South Africa	52
German FR	52	India	12
Australia	27	Botswana	4
Poland	27	Mongolia	3?
UK	5		
Canada	2	World	515

Main source: United Nations, *Energy Statistics Yearbook* (1982).

Table 2.7   Proven oil reserves at the end of 1984 in thousands of millions of tonnes and life of reserves in years at current rate of extraction (* over 100 years)

	Developing countries					Developed countries		
	Proven oil reserves	Life of reserves		Proven oil reserves	Life of reserves		Proven oil reserves	Life of reserves
Saudi Arabia	23.0	*	Venezuela	3.7	38	USSR	8.6	14
Kuwait	12.4	*	Libya	2.8	52	USA	4.4	9
Mexico	6.8	45	China	2.6	23	UK	1.8	14
Iran	6.6	61	Nigeria	2.3	33	Norway	1.1	32
Iraq	6.0	*	Indonesia	1.2	17	Canada	1.1	15
Abu Dhabi	4.0	*	Algeria	1.2	27	World	96.1	34

Source: British Petroleum, *BP Statistical Review of World Energy* (June 1985).

reserves and have probably been explored more intensively than the developing countries. The life of the reserves of the developed countries with oil is short. They consume most of the world's oil. Japan and most West and East European countries have virtually no oil reserves at all.

As can be seen in table 2.7, twelve developing countries each have over about one per cent of the world's oil reserves, while many others have smaller amounts. In all the developing countries listed in table 2.7, oil companies based in the developed countries were responsible for discovering oil and then extracting and transporting it. Gradually the influence of the host countries has increased so that now most oil industries are state owned (e.g. Pemex in Mexico), but foreign oil companies remain generally as contractors. With the sharp rises in oil prices in 1973–4, and again in the late 1970s, oil-producing countries (including the United Kingdom) have received much more for crude oil and its products *relative* to other products than they did. As a result, the producers have been able to cut output, ensuring a longer life for their reserves. Unfortunately for the numerous developing countries with little or no oil of their own the price they pay for oil imports has risen greatly.

Natural gas is much less important than oil in international trade. Deposits are more concentrated in distribution than are oil deposits. The Soviet Union alone has 43 per cent of all world reserves but is exporting natural gas at present only to Eastern and Western Europe, by pipeline. The Middle East has about 25 per cent, most in Iran. The United States has already used most of its known reserves. Only locally is natural gas of some importance in developing countries.

Without coal or oil reserves, most developing countries have lost out in the drive to use fossil fuels to provide energy for modern industry. They cannot afford to import much coal or oil. They have to use fuelwood for some purposes and still depend heavily on work animals. The animals' dung, which should be returned to the land as manure, may be used as fuel. The collection of fuelwood threatens large areas of forest and woodland in the developing world. Thus the forests of the developing world are not only being cleared for cultivation, because of the pressure on land, or cut for construction timber and raw materials, but are also being cut for fuelwood.

There is now much concern in the world about the clearance of forests. Some forests, especially the tropical rain forest and forests in dry areas, cannot easily be replaced at all. In other areas, if they are cut, they should be replanted carefully, a procedure so far followed extensively in only a few countries, most notably perhaps in Japan.

As stressed earlier in the book, you should always regard numerical data with suspicion. Alarm is expressed in many quarters about the depletion of the world's forests, yet the following FAO figures seem to put in doubt the seriousness of the trend. The figures are for the area of forest in the world in millions of hectares: 1963, 4169; 1970, 4157; 1975, 4164; 1982, 4090.

It is widely agreed that with time it will be necessary to make much greater use of sources of fuel other than fossil fuels or fuelwood. Here the developed countries of the world are showing the way. With its new nuclear power stations France is producing comparatively cheap electricity. In Japan you will see many homes with solar panels in the roof. The developed countries have the scientists and engineers, as well as the capital, to experiment with and apply new sources, the developing ones mostly do not. If they are lucky (or unlucky?) they will get capital and technical help from the developed ones.

Where are the reserves of energy that are not fossil fuels? Uranium deposits are found in many countries but, perhaps through more intensive exploration for minerals, at present most of the known uranium is in the developed countries (United States of America, Soviet Union, Canada, Australia). Western Europe and Japan have very little and France obtains uranium from Niger and other former colonies in Africa. The hydroelectric potential in the world as a whole is very large but much of it is in areas that are difficult to reach (the Andes, south-west China, northern Siberia) or where the electricity could not at present be absorbed (the Amazon and Congo basins). Solar energy can be used locally at present but eventually could be fed into electricity transmission systems. Developing countries have limited technological backup to maintain the delicate small- or large-scale units. The advantage of fossil fuels is that they can be transported long distances. Nuclear and hydro power must be in the form of electricity. Most developing countries have only very limited systems for transmitting electricity.

For the next few decades there is apparently 'enough' oil and natural gas in the world, so long as the developing countries remain low consumers of fossil fuels. Additional potential sources of energy are hydrocarbons in oil shales and tar sands, hardly extracted yet, and possible deep-earth gas of non-organic origin. The technology and capital needed to extract such minerals are beyond the reach of developing countries at present.

Non-fuel mineral reserves

The bioclimatic resources of the world feed the human population and provide some raw materials and fuel. The fossil fuels provide most of the fuel and power used in the world and also raw materials. Non-fuel minerals provide only raw materials. The direct use of most of them in the economic

LIMA, VIERNES 4 DE SETIEMBRE DE 1981

Ya es hora de aprovechar nuestras riquezas

Figure 2.2 Large gold reserves found in Peru. Now is the time to make use of our riches. (The cartoon refers to a saying attributed to a nineteenth-century Italian visitor to Peru, A. Raimondi: 'Peru is a beggar sitting on a seat of gold.') *Source: El Comercio* (4 September 1981).

life of developing countries is rather limited. Although developing countries have the main reserves of some non-fuel minerals they lack the industrial capacity to transform them into manufactured products.

Data for about eighty different non-fuel minerals are included in the US Bureau of Mines publication *Mineral Facts and Problems* (1980). Some, like sand, lime and salt, are found very widely. Others are highly concentrated in their location. All are used commercially in one way or another but some are much more important than others.

Since non-fuel minerals are used for such a wide variety of purposes and in such different quantities, there is no point in trying to compare their importance according to weight. For example, 1000 million tonnes of iron ore are extracted each year in the world, with an iron content of about half that weight but only about 1000 tonnes of gold (a million kilograms) are extracted.

Given the difficulty of using weight to assess reserves comparatively, the scores for each country for each of fifteen important minerals are shown as percentages of the proved world total of reserves of each mineral in table 2.8. The five countries each given their own columns are those with the most non-fuel minerals. Together they have only 12 per cent of the population of the world but nearly 60 per cent of the proved reserves of the minerals

Table 2.8   Non-fuel mineral reserves by country *c.* 1980 expressed as percentages of the world total of each item

			Countries with large reserves				
		USSR	*South Africa*	*Canada*	*Australia*	*USA*	*Other sources*
1	Iron	30	1	12	12	4	Brazil 17, India 6
2	Manganese	26	53	0	9	0	Gabon 5
3	Nickel	14	0	15	9	1	New Caledonia 25
4	Chromium	1	68	0	0	0	Zimbabwe 30
5	Aluminium	2	0	0	18	1	Guinea 29, Brazil 11
6	Copper	9	0	7	5	19	Chile 20
7	Zinc	7	7	19	10	9	Brazil 6
8	Lead	13	4	9	14	21	Mexico 4
9	Tin	10	0	0	4	1	Indonesia 16, China 16
10	Silver	20	0	20	13	19	Mexico 13
11	Gold	24	51	1	4	4	Philippines 2
12	Potash	44	0	30	0	3	German FR 5
13	Phosphates	13	9	1	0	5	Morocco 53
14	Sulphur	14	0	14	1	10	Iran 8, Poland 8
15	Industrial diamonds	4	7	0	0	0	Zaire 74

Source: Bureau of Mines, *Mineral Facts and Problems* (1980)

included in this assessment. In the rest of the world Western Europe and Japan are large consumers of mineral raw materials but have few reserves, while some areas of the developing world have large reserves of particular minerals (see table 2.8 for examples).

As noted, the use in manufacturing of non-fuel minerals, especially of metal, is limited in the developing countries. Some countries, such as Mexico, Brazil, Venezuela, India and China, use their own iron ore to produce iron and steel. Bauxite, ferro-alloys such as manganese and chromium, and non-ferrous metals, such as copper, lead and zinc, are almost all sent to the developed countries as primary products, processed only, mainly by refining to reduce weight for shipment.

The exploration for minerals in some parts of the world has slowed down recently. Mining companies based in the industrial economies have preferred to invest in countries regarded as stable politically, such as Australia and Canada. In the developing world, southern Africa, South-east Asia (Vietnam conflict until the mid-1970s) and, of course, the Middle East have been regarded as particularly risky, whereas Latin America has remained fairly attractive. But the governments of developing countries are faced by the same dilemma over the use of their non-fuel minerals as of their fossil fuels. Should they wait until they can use their own minerals? If they wait too long the industrial countries may find substitutes and the minerals that are valuable now might not be wanted.

Key ideas

1 Natural resources may be bioclimatic or mineral, fixed or flow, exhaustible or inexhaustible.
2 Arable land has gradually increased in extent over time, but in recent decades the reduced rate of increase has caused concern.
3 Agricultural yields can be increased by double cropping, irrigation, greenhouses and fertilizers.
4 Fossil fuels provide most of the world energy but in time non-fossil fuels will increasingly have to be used. With these developed countries are already at a technological advantage.
5 Third World countries have major reserves of non-fuel minerals but limited capacity to make them into manufactured products.

3
Production and consumption of goods and services

Labour productivity in agriculture

Until the nineteenth century virtually all work in agriculture was carried out by people themselves or with the help of work animals. Either way, most of the population worked full or part of the time on the land, and the animals, while a help, were also a liability, needing (unlike tractors) to be fed even when not being used. It is not surprising then that, once steam-driven machinery could be adapted, it was welcomed to do some work, such as threshing. The internal combustion engine has proved much more flexible than the steam engine.

I have taken many visitors from developing countries round the British countryside and invariably they remark on how few people there are working the land. The crops seem to look after themselves. One of the most remarkable changes in the world economy in modern times has been the shift of labour from the agricultural sector to other sectors. The data in table 3.1 show that in the United Kingdom and United States only 2 per cent of the economically active population works in agriculture. Among the developed countries Romania and Yugoslavia have more than a third of their labour force still in agriculture, but in North America, Australia, Japan and West Europe the percentage is mostly well below 10 per cent. In contrast there are a number of countries in Africa and Asia where about 90 per cent are engaged in the agricultural sector (see plates 3.1 and 3.2).

Will the developing countries follow the path of the developed ones and end up eventually with only a few per cent of their labour force in

Plates 3.1 and 3.2   Two scenes from China. Both illustrate the commonly found phenomenon of over-manning or underemployment: the movement of sand near Guilin (1980) and a team of barrowmen near Nanjing (1982). The latter may be cheaper and more convenient to hire than a lorry. The proverb 'Many hands (or Hans) make light work' comes to mind here, though with reservations.

Table 3.1 Economically active population in agriculture as a percentage of total economically active population in selected countries in 1983

High		Middle		Low	
Nepal	92	India	60	USSR	14
Rwanda	88	China	56	Argentina	12
Mali	85	Nigeria	50	Japan	9
Bangladesh	83	Philippines	43	Australia	5
Tanzania	79	Brazil	35	USA	2
Ethiopia	77	Mexico	33	UK	2

Source: Food and Agriculture Organization, *Production Yearbook* (1984).

agriculture? The data in table 3.2 show how long it took some of the now developed countries to reach their current levels. You can see from the data that Britain must already have become very highly industrialized by 1850, whereas the United States was still very agricultural. The data show also that in the last century present-day developed countries had similar percentages of workers in agriculture to many developing countries now.

Table 3.2 Economically active population in agriculture and associated activities as a percentage of total economically active population in selected developed countries 1850–83

	Great Britain*	France	USA	Japan	Australia
1850	22	52	64		
1870	15	50	50		
1890	11	45	43	82	
1910	9	41	32	63	24
1930	6	36	22	49	21
1950	5	27	12	48	14
1970	3	14	4	21	8
1984	2	7	2	9	5

Note: * Great Britain (excluding Ireland) to 1910, thereafter United Kingdom
Source: P. Bairoch and others, 'The working population and its structure', *Statistiques Internationales Retrospectives* (University of Brussels), vol. 1, table A2.

Yields in agriculture

In chapter 2 it was shown that the area of arable land in the world has not been extended greatly in the last forty years. Much of the increase that has taken place has been at the expense of forest, especially in Brazil, where both tropical and southern pine forest areas have been cleared. In the 1950s large areas of grassland were brought into use in the Soviet Union.

The United States is one of the most fortunate countries in the world because in the early 1980s the 160 million ha in actual crop production, about 17 per cent of the total national land area (including Alaska), could be extended if necessary by 60 million ha. As it is, the United States now provides a huge surplus of agricultural products for export ($40 bn. in value, enough to pay for 60 per cent of its oil imports). There are about 70 ha of land under crops per one hundred people in the United States. In contrast, in China there are only about 10 hectares per hundred people and no further large potential. In China new areas of cultivation are painstakingly acquired in various ways: terracing of steep hillsides, levelling of uneven ground, reclamation of marshes, local irrigation projects. There comes a point when the slope becomes too steep even to be terraced. Very large transfers of water from one river basin to another have been proposed in China, but the construction work needed would be complicated and costly.

New cultivable land is hard to create in many countries and it is not surprising that the use of fertilizers has become very widespread in some developing countries as well as in most developed ones. According to *World Development Report 1985* (table 3.6), in just twelve years the level of fertilizer consumption per hectare of arable land in low income countries, defined as those with less than US$400 per inhabitant in 1983, rose more than three times. However this was uneven, with a very big increase in China and South Asia (India, Bangladesh, Pakistan) but not much in Africa south of the Sahara.

Tables 3.3–3.5 show yields of wheat, rice and maize, the three cereals produced in the largest quantities in the world as a whole (1983 world totals in millions of tonnes: wheat 498, rice 450, maize 344). These and other cereals make a major contribution to the food intake of humans in most parts of the world and maize is also widely fed to livestock. They are of great importance, therefore, in world food production. Study the data in the tables carefully and then consider the following points.

1   Would the 1981–3 data be more meaningful if the three yield values were averaged?
2   Are you surprised (or impressed) by the general increases in yields in the last thirty-five years?
3   Why do yields vary so greatly among countries?

Table 3.3 Wheat yields in selected countries in hundreds of kilograms per hectare

	1948–52	1961–5	1974–6	1981	1982	1983	1984
UK	27	41	44	58	62	64	77
Mexico	9	19	37	37	44	37	39
USA	11	17	20	23	24	27	26
World	10	12	17	19	20	22	23
India	7	8	13	16	17	18	19
USSR	8	10	14	14	15	16	15
Ethiopia	4	7	10	10	13	13	11

Source: Food and Agriculture Organization, *Production Yearbook* (various numbers to 1984).

Table 3.4 Rice yields in selected countries in hundreds of kilograms per hectare

	1948–52	1961–5	1974–6	1981	1982	1983	1984
Italy	49	51	54	53	54	59	58
Japan	40	50	58	56	57	57	64
China	22	28	35	43	49	51	53
World	16	21	25	28	30	31	32
Pakistan	14*	14	23	26	26	26	21
Philippines	12	13	17	24	24	25	25
India	11	15	17	20	19	22	21
Bangladesh	14*	15	18	20	20	20	20
Thailand	13	18	18	20	19	20	20

Note: * data only for whole of former Pakistan
Source: Food and Agriculture Organization, *Production Yearbook* (various numbers to 1984).

Table 3.5 Maize yields in selected countries in hundreds of kilograms per hectare

	1948–52	1961–5	1974–6	1981	1982	1983	1984
Italy	18	33	44	59	69	66	70
USA	25	42	52	69	72	51	67
World	16	22	27	35	36	28	35
Brazil	12	13	15	18	17	17	17
Venezuela	10	11	12	15	16	17	17
Mexico	8	11	12	18	18	17	16
Kenya	13	11	16	13	19	12	12
South Africa	8	13	15	30	18	10	11
Nigeria	9	6	8	9	10	9	8

Source: Food and Agriculture Organization, *Production Yearbook* (various numbers to 1984).

4   With reference to wheat, why are UK yields more than twice as high as US yields and four times Soviet yields? What happens in Mexico? Australian wheat yields are similar to those in the Soviet Union.
5   With reference to all three cereals, can the countries with the lowest yields raise these to the levels reached in the countries with the highest yields?
6   Is there a limit to which yields can be raised?

It will probably have occurred to you that yields vary through various influences. Some farmland has better natural conditions of soil, water and heat than other farmland. More fertilizers are applied in some areas than in others. Land tenure or ownership may also have something to do with the enthusiasm with which farmers work their land. Do you think that mechanization affects yields? What other consequences come from mechanization? Some data have already been given on the use of fertilizers. Table 3.6 contains data for all the countries included in tables 3.3–3.5, which show yields of wheat, rice and maize. They will help you further to appreciate the great differences in the use of fertilizers in the world. How far do they go in explaining differences in yield?

Table 3.6 Use of fertilizer in hundreds of grams of plant nutrient per hectare of arable land

Japan	4,121	South Africa	831	India	346
UK	3,647	Mexico	778	Kenya	289
Italy	1,614	Pakistan	616	Philippines	288
China	1,575	Bangladesh	512	Thailand	183
USA	867*	Venezuela	408	Nigeria	65
USSR	867*	Brazil	365	Ethiopia	26

Note: * same figure, by coincidence
Source: World Bank, *World Development Report* (1985), table 6.

Industry

As labour has been released from the agricultural sector through mechanization, people have been able to move into other activities. A distinction is made in other sectors between industry and services. The industrial sector produces goods such as steel and cloth, the service sector includes 'non-goods' activities such as health care, finance and entertainment. Industry can have a broader meaning than just manufacturing. It usually includes processing (such as sugar refining), and in some countries (e.g. Soviet Union) mining. Occasionally the term even includes agriculture.

The division between industry and services is not all that clear but in the Soviet Union and the East European countries industry (including mining and transport) is regarded as a more 'worthy' and 'productive' sector than services. In the market economy industrial countries services are considered to be just as essential as agriculture and industry and contribute to gross national product. The terms 'primary,' 'secondary' and 'tertiary' sectors are commonly used as follows:

Primary: agriculture, forestry, fishing and extractive (mining and quarrying) producing goods directly from natural resources.

Secondary: processing and manufacturing, transforming some of the products of the Primary sector. Sometimes includes extractive.

Tertiary: non-goods, but further subdivided sometimes to recognize a Quaternary sector of workers servicing the other sectors.

It is as well to appreciate that the fine distinctions noted above exist in developed countries of different ideological systems. In most developing countries the problem of industry is much more down-to-earth. The task has been to develop from almost nothing at least some industrial capacity using modern means of production (inanimate sources of energy, electricity, machinery). It was pointed out in chapter 1 that until quite recently the colonial countries had been regarded by the industrial countries as sources of food, fuel and raw materials, to be sold manufactured goods in return. The extent to which this arrangement and image are no longer true will be shown in chapter 4.

Industrialization has been widely seen by leaders of developing countries as an advantage, and there are several reasons why. First, the exchange of products in the past has been in favour of the manufacturing countries because they can add a large degree of 'value' to the primary products they import. Second, the import of manufactured goods by developing countries could be cut by 'import substitution'; consumer manufactures, a major item of import in many developing countries, though largely destined for the few well-off citizens there, could be made at home. Finally, producer goods should also be manufactured in order that the country should become more independent; each country should have a heavy industrial base.

Some countries have already followed the above path. A hundred years ago, both Russia and Japan were 'developing' countries of the time (the term was not used until much later), with 80–90 per cent of their labour force in agriculture. Each now has a wide range of industries, producer and consumer, with engineering being particularly important. More recently India, China, Brazil, Argentina and Mexico have developed considerable industrial capacities, thanks to their large population sizes.

A problem for many developing countries aspiring to industrialize is that their economies are very small. Some industries need to be of a certain size to function successfully. The economies of small steel mills and oil refineries have improved, and cement and textile factories, for example, do not need to be very large. On the other hand, the manufacture of motor vehicles and aircraft, of many other kinds of machinery and equipment, and of computers and associated information-technology equipment, does seem to depend on a large market. The small developing countries also lack people to carry out research into science and technology and are short of highly skilled labour.

The contrasts in the world in the 1980s with regard to the relative importance of the three sectors, agriculture, industry and services, are brought out in table 3.7. Note that the figures are only percentages and they do not show the total sizes of the economies. Again, they show the contribution of the total value of gross domestic product (GDP) made to each sector but are not the same percentages as for the division of the labour force. This is because in most countries more GDP is 'produced' per worker in industry and in services than per worker in agriculture. The contribution of the agricultural sector may, however, be understated because a large part of the produce is used locally and not necessarily fully recorded. The same, however, is true of many services in developed countries, part of the growing 'black economy'.

Manufacturing is a subset of all industry, which also includes mining, construction, electricity, water and gas. Mining is clearly an important sector in some countries and regions, especially the high-income oil exporters of the Middle East. Manufacturing is regarded by the World Bank as 'typically the most dynamic part of the industrial sector' (*World Development Report*, 1985) (see table 3.7).

From the data in the table it is clear that, as we might have expected, in the period 1965–83 the share of GDP provided by agriculture has universally declined. The data for manufacturing show a newer trend, the relative decline in its importance too. Services, on the other hand, have increased almost everywhere.

The distribution of industrial capacity and production in the world can be measured in various ways. Two very rough but clearly understood guides to differences in the level of industrialization among the countries of the world are used here, the consumption of energy and the production of steel. In order to make direct comparison of countries, straightforward values per inhabitant are given in table 3.8.

Only some of the energy consumed in the world is used in industry, about 60 per cent in the Soviet Union, for example. Heating, transport and agriculture use some, particularly in developed countries (mostly in colder latitudes and with much private motoring). Even when allowance is made for other users, a large gap can be seen (table 3.8) between levels in a selection of developed countries and in a larger selection of developing ones. The very high level in North America reflects to some extent the use of large cars, while the high level in the Soviet Union and some East European countries

Table 3.7   The structure of production showing the distribution of gross domestic product by sectors in percentages in the largest countries of the world (data not available for the USSR, Vietnam or France)

Country	Agriculture		Industry				Services	
			Total		Manufactures subsection			
	1965	1983	1965	1983	1965	1983	1965	1983
China	40	37	38	45	NA	NA	22	18
India	47	36	22	26	15	15	31	38
USA	3	2	38	32	29	21	59	66
Indonesia	59	26	12	39	8	13	29	35
Brazil	19	12	33	35	26	27	48	53
Japan	9	4	43	42	32	30	48	55
Bangladesh	53	47	11	13	NA	NA	36	40
Pakistan	40	27	20	27	14	19	40	46
Nigeria	53	26	19	34	7	5	29	40
Mexico	14	8	31	40	21	22	54	52
German FR	NA	2	NA	46	NA	36	NA	52
Italy	11	6	41	40	NA	NA	48	54
UK	3	2	41	32	30	18	56	66
Philippines	26	22	28	36	20	25	46	42
Thailand	35	23	23	27	14	19	42	50
Turkey	34	19	25	33	16	24	41	48
Egypt	29	20	27	33	NA	NA	45	47
Groups of countries								
Low-income	43	37	29	34	14	14	28	29
Middle-income	21	15	31	36	20	21	47	49
Upper-middle-income	17	11	35	37	22	24	49	52
High-income								
oil exporters	5	2	65	65	5	6	30	33
Industrial market	5	3	39	35	29	24	56	62

Key: NA = not available.
Source: World Bank, *World Development Report* (1985).

reflects the emphasis on heavy industry and lack of regard for efficiency in use (now admitted in the Soviet press and to be corrected). Western Europe and Japan depend heavily on imported fuel (unlike the Soviet Union or Canada) and for this reason are more concerned with economizing.

When you have thought about the use of energy in the industrial countries, you might consider whether the developing countries could reach comparable levels. By what multiple would they have to increase, even to reach the level in Japan? The problem is more complicated than it looks because the population in most of them is growing rapidly.

Table 3.8 Consumption of commercial sources of energy in kilograms of coal equivalent per inhabitant

High		Moderate to low		Very low	
Canada	9,700	Colombia	900	Mozambique	100
USA	9,430	Brazil	700	Sudan	90
German DR	7,390	Egypt	620	Zaire	70
USSR	5,770	China	580	Burma	70
German FR	5,510	Philippines	330	Bangladesh	50
UK	4,540	Indonesia	230	Ethiopia	30
Japan	3,500	India	200	Nepal	10

Source: United Nations, *Energy Statistics Yearbook* (1982), table 1.

Table 3.9 Production of steel in kilograms per inhabitant in selected countries, early 1980s

High		Moderate to low		Little or none	
Belgium	1,230	Korean Republic	152	Bangladesh	2
Czechoslovakia	990	Mexico	103	Indonesia	0
Japan	950	Brazil	84	Vietnam	0
German FR	720	Chile	62	Nigeria	0
Canada	660	China	38	Pakistan	0
USSR	560	India	14	Ethiopia	0

Source: United Nations, *Statistical Yearbook* (1980–1).

Steel is one of the most important industrial products in the world in value and in the variety of products made from it. Steel production (see table 3.9) has therefore been taken as a rough guide to the level of heavy industrial production in various countries. A century ago the UK and USA would have been near the top of the list in iron and steel produced per inhabitant. Now, with 200 and 460 kg respectively, they are quite a long way down. All the high-level countries in the table export some of the steel they produce in processed or manufactured form. Even from the selection of countries given in table 3.9 it is evident that some developing countries have steel industries. On the other hand, most developing countries produce none at all, including some that are large in population.

Services

The term services is used rather loosely to cover a number of sectors and activities. These affect the well-being of the population and also the capability of the economy to become more industrialized, mechanized, sophisticated and productive. Examine the data in table 3.10 and then think about the following points (numbers relate to columns in the table):

1 The definition of literacy is not a precise one (a precise definition, for example, would be having a telephone at home or not). Standards used to determine whether a person is literate or not must vary greatly from country to country, and only people over an appropriate age can be asked. While nearly everyone can speak, many people in developing

Table 3.10 Selected indicators of services and living standards in the twenty largest countries of the world in population

	1	*2*	*3*	*4*	*5*	*6*
			Infant	*Life expectancy*		
	Literacy	*Research*	*mortality*	*at birth*	*Telephones*	*GNP*
China	60	7	38	65	1	290
India	42	4	118	53	1	260
USSR	98	280	32	69	9	6,350
USA	99	267	11	75	79	14,090
Indonesia	68	5	87	55	0	560
Brazil	73	18	71	63	7	1,890
Japan	99	348	6	77	48	10,100
Bangladesh	31	2	133	48	0	130
Pakistan	29	4	120	50	0	390
Nigeria	30	2	105	50	1	760
Mexico	84	8	53	66	8	2,240
German FR	99	182	10	74	49	11,420
Vietnam	40	22	90	66	0	250
Italy	96	67	12	74	36	6,350
Philippines	89	7	50	64	2	760
UK	99	139	10	73	50	9,050
France	99	129	9	75	50	10,390
Thailand	88	12	51	63	1	810
Turkey	66	18	110	63	5	1,230
Egypt	42	23	80	57	1	700
World	NA	59	81	62	12	2,760

Key: 1 population over an eligible age able to read as a percentage of all such population (substantially different values are given in the United Nations *Statistical Yearbook* (1982)).

2 scientists and engineers engaged in research and experimental development per 100,000 total population

3 deaths of infants under the age of one year per thousand live births

4 average life expectancy in years at birth

5 telephones in use per 100 inhabitants in 1981

6 gross national product in US dollars per inhabitant

Sources: 1 *World's Children Data Sheet* (1982).

2 and 5 United Nations, *Statistical Yearbook* (various years).

3, 4 and 6 Population Reference Bureau, *World Population Data Sheet* (1985).

countries are unable to read, whereas in all developed countries nearly a 100 per cent literacy is claimed. It is probably harder to learn to read and write in some languages than in others, Spanish being easier than Chinese, for example, because the former has near-phonetic letters, while the Chinese has basically non-phonetic characters.

What are the advantages of being able to read and write? At worst, if you cannot read, you would find life difficult getting round in a big city. You might be persuaded by a fraud to sign something you did not understand. In the countryside you could not read the instructions on a bag of fertilizers or about how to use and service a machine. More importantly, from the point of view of the overall development of your country, until you had reached a certain educational level, it would not be possible to judge whether you might be suitable to become a professional worker and perhaps in some way contribute to research.

2 Research in science and technology is essential for development. To be sure, much research is in effect wasted because it is duplicated. Much effort also goes into military research, the economic benefits of which are incidental and not its primary aim. Even so the following fact is disturbing for the developing countries: these have (including China) about 75 per cent of the total population of the world and about 300,000 scientists and engineers engaged in research and experimental development. A large number, you may think. Not so when you find that the remaining 25 per cent of the world's population has about 2.5 million. Japan alone claims over 400,000, while the Soviet Union claims over 1.5 million, but as Soviet definitions are often over generous I have cut that to half in the Soviet entry in table 3.10.

In column 2 of table 3.10 the development gap stands out very clearly. So does the fact that Western Europe seems to lag far behind the Soviet Union, United States and Japan. The 'research gap', as I think we can call it, will be a difficult one to narrow, let alone close. Higher educational establishments are turning out scientists and engineers as fast as they can in developed countries. Both state and private companies absorb them and provide funds for their work. Given the great backwardness of most developing countries in so many respects, already illustrated by many data sets in this book, surely the developing countries need the research. As it is, most innovations start in a developed country and find their way, either through deliberate transfer, or by accident, into developing countries.

3 The availability of modern health care is regarded as highly desirable in virtually every country. It can be measured, as in earlier tables, by the availability of physicians or, with fairly similar results, by the availability of hospital beds. In table 3.10 infant mortality and life expectancy rates are used because, after all, the idea of health care is to keep people alive

as long as possible. Most developing countries and even some developed ones have a long way to go to reach the low level of 6 infant deaths per thousand live births achieved by Japan in the early 1980s. The nearer the index approaches zero, the more difficult it must become to drop another unit per thousand. If, however, infant mortality rates, and of course those for children of all ages, are lowered, there will be more women after two or three decades have passed to bear more children.

4   Life expectancy is a measure often used to illustrate the quality of life in a country. Levels throughout the world have tended to creep up in the last few decades. A drop might be expected in local areas where a war or acute famine alters the situation. The ex-British colonies of Gambia, with 35 years and Sierra Leone, with 34 years, have the lowest life expectancy rates given in the 1985 *World Population Data Sheet*, and the 37 years recorded for Afghanistan is also very low. The problem of care of the elderly is likely to become acute in the decades to come, not only in the developed countries but in some developing ones as well. Chinese planners, for example, know that if they do enforce their very drastic family planning programme to reduce the number of births, then in a few decades' time there could be one grandchild supporting two or even four grandparents.

5   While the telephone is widely regarded as a necessity in developed countries, as well as an object of both amusement and irritation, its use in most developing countries is very restricted. Given the importance attached to information in the developed world, the telephone and associated means of rapid transfer of information must be taken seriously in developing countries. The score of zero against several countries in column 5 of table 3.10 means that they have so few telephones in relation to population that, when expressed per 100 inhabitants, the figure rounds down to 0 rather than up to 1. In developing countries the telephone users, whether public or private, are highly concentrated in the larger cities.

Someone said that development is indivisible (you might think it invisible in some of the poorest countries). What the statement means is that you cannot have some sectors of your economy developed and some not developed. If there are plenty of doctors, there will be plenty of hospitals and also good educational, transport and other facilities. To what extent do the data sets in this chapter support the view of indivisible development?

Case study D

Fuelwood

Dwindling reserves of petroleum and artful tampering with its distribution are the stuff of which headlines are made. Yet for more than a third of the world's people, the real energy crisis is a daily scramble to find the wood they need to cook dinner. Their search for wood, once a simple chore and now, as forests recede, a day's labor in some places, has been strangely neglected by diplomats, economists, and the media. But the firewood crisis will be making news – one way or another – for the rest of the century.

While chemists devise ever more sophisticated uses for wood, including cellophane and rayon, at least half of all the timber cut in the world still fulfills its original role for humans – as fuel for cooking and, in colder mountain regions, a source of warmth. Nine-tenths of the people in most poor countries today depend on firewood as their chief source of fuel. And all too often, the growth in human population is outpacing the growth of new trees – not surprising when the average user burns as much as a ton of firewood a year. The results are soaring wood prices, a growing drain on incomes and physical energies in order to satisfy basic fuel needs, a costly diversion of animal manures to cooking food rather than producing it, and an ecologically disastrous spread of treeless landscapes.

The firewood crisis is probably most acute today in the countries of the densely populated Indian subcontinent, and in the semi-arid stretches of central Africa fringing the Sahara Desert, though it plagues many other regions as well. In Latin America, for example, the scarcity of wood and charcoal is a problem throughout most of the Andean region, Central America, and the Caribbean. (p. 5)

Village politics can undermine a program as well. An incident from Ethiopia a few years back presents an extreme case, but its lessons are plain. A rural reforestation program was initiated as a public works scheme to help control erosion and supply local wood needs. The planting jobs were given to the local poor, mostly landless laborers who badly needed the low wages they could earn in the planting program. Seedlings were distributed, planting commenced, and all seemed to be going well – until the overseers journeyed out to check the progress. They found that in many areas the seedlings had been planted upside down! The laborers, of course, well knew the difference between roots and branches; they also knew that given the feudal land-tenure system in which they were living,

Table D.1 Relationships between forest area, roundwood (= timber) and fuelwood use

	1 Population (millions)	2 Forest area (million ha)	3 Roundwood (million m³)	4 Fuelwood (million m³)	5 6 Fuelwood (tonnes of coal equivalent) 1970 1981		7 kg of fuelwood in tce per ha forest	8 m³ of fuelwood as % of m³ roundwood
Asia	2,672	557	1,017	701	218	272	490	70
Africa	499	691	434	410	98	132	190	94
South America	252	933	315	216	64	85	90	69
North America	387	681	531	147	17	21	30	28
USSR	270	920	356	81	29	26	30	23
Europe	488	155	334	55	23	21	140	16
World*	4,591	4,090	3,020	1,616	451	560	140	54

Note: * excludes Australia and New Zealand
Sources: Food and Agriculture Organization, *Production Yearbook* (1983); United Nations, *Energy Statistics Yearbook* (1982); United Nations, *Statistical Yearbook* (1981), table 103.

Case study D (*continued*)

most of the benefits of the planting would flow one way or another into the hands of their lords. They were not anxious to work efficiently for substandard wages on a project that brought them few personal returns. (p. 16)

Fuelwood, a serious threat to the forests of the world

Study tables D.1 and D.2. Table D.1 has data for continents (plus the Soviet Union, but excluding Australia and New Zealand which use little fuelwood). You can compare the area of forest (2) in the early 1980s with population (1) and also roundwood (3) (for construction and raw material)

Table D.2   Fuelwood as a serious threat to the forests in some countries

	1 *Forest area* *(million ha)*	*2* *Fuelwood* *in millions* *m³ collected,* *1982*	*3* *kg fuelwood* *collected per* *ha forest,* *1982*
Bangladesh	2.1	30	14,290
Kenya	2.5	27	10,800
Pakistan	2.9	18	6,710
Nigeria	14.3	76	5,315
India	67.5	209	3,100
Philippines	12.2	28	2,300
Thailand	15.8	35	2,220
Vietnam	10.2	20	1,960
China	128.2	157	1,225
Ethiopia	26.5	27	1,020
Indonesia	121.8	112	920
Tanzania	41.9	37	883
Turkey	20.2	15	743
Sudan	48.3	35	725
USA	284.5	99	348
Mexico	47.4	13	274
Brazil	570.0	170	208
Zaire	177.0	28	158
Canada	326.0	5	15

Sources: Food and Agriculture Organization, *Production Yearbook*, and United Nations, *Energy Statistics Yearbook*.

Case study D (*continued*)

and fuelwood (4). In columns 5 and 6 fuelwood is expressed in tonnes of coal equivalent instead of cubic metres. Why does the ratio of one to the other differ from one region to another? Can you think why (see column 8) much more fuelwood is collected in relation to roundwood in developing countries than in developed ones?

In table D2 you will see that forest is being cleared for fuelwood far more quickly in some countries than in others. What do the differences tell us about the countries listed and the question of development in general? Should the use of wood for fuel be banned? How realistic would such a law be in practice?

Note that the density of forest (and therefore the biomass per hectare) varies greatly from place to place. Note also that, as fuelwood is not generally transported far, the cutting of wood for this purpose may have a much more drastic effect in some parts of a country than in others.

Source: Eckholm, E. (1975) 'The other energy crisis: firewood', *Worldwatch Paper 1*, Washington DC, Worldwatch Institute.

Key ideas

1 In developed countries the proportion of the workforce engaged in agriculture has declined during the last century; developing countries seek to emulate this trend but at the present time proportions employed in agriculture are high.
2 Yields in agriculture are increasing as a result of the application of capital to agriculture.
3 Labour has moved from agriculture into industry and services.

4
International transactions

The structure of international trade by countries

The importance of foreign trade to the economy of a country can be judged approximately by comparing the value of either total trade or imports only (import coefficient) with total gross national product (GNP). The import coefficient varies greatly from country to country but is very low for the four largest countries in the world in population, China, India, the Soviet Union and the United States of America. These are so large that they are able to be more self-sufficient than most other countries. The coefficient is between 20–25 per cent in some countries of Western Europe, but very high in Hong Kong and Singapore. It is quite high in most developing countries.

The structure of the foreign trade of a selection of developed and developing countries is examined in tables 4.1 and 4.2. In table 4.1 nineteen selected countries are arranged according to the percentages of their total exports made up of primary products and of manufactured goods. The United Nations *Yearbook of International Trade Statistics* has data for ten classes of exports. The distinction between primary products and secondary ones is not clear cut and columns 1–4 include processed items. The bias may therefore give too much weight to primary products. In the *Yearbook* imports are only divided into five classes. The first three are mainly primary products, the last two secondary. Unfortunately comparable data are not available in the United Nations *Yearbook of International Trade Statistics* for the Soviet Union, China, Cuba or South Africa.

Look carefully at the data in the two tables. Then make a note of any

Table 4.1 The exports of nineteen selected countries in percentages of total value (most for 1981)

	1–4 (mainly primary products raw or processed)	5–10 (mainly secondary products)	1 Agriculture	2 Extractive manufacture	3 Food manufacture	4 Metals	5 Textiles	6 Wood/paper	7 Chemicals	8 Non-metal	9 Metal manufacture	10 Other manufacture
Japan	13	87	—	—	1	12	4	1	8	1	70	3
Czechoslovakia (1980)	16	84	2	3	3	8	10	3	9	2	59	1
USA	26	74	14	5	5	2	2	4	14	1	51	2
UK	32	68	2	19	6	5	5	2	17	1	40	4
Bangladesh (1978)	36	63	34	—	2	—	59	1	2	—	—	1
Canada	38	62	10	17	4	7	1	15	8	1	36	2
India	49	51	25	15	8	1	30	—	5	1	12	—
Brazil	58	42	16	12	24	6	7	4	11	1	19	1
New Zealand	70	30	14	1	50	5	11	7	5	1	6	1
Argentina	71	29	40	—	25	6	7	1	13	1	8	1
Peru	75	25	8	33	7	27	9	—	12	1	2	1
Australia	75	25	24	26	16	9	2	1	12	—	6	3
Venezuela	84	16	—	81	—	3	—	—	15	—	1	—
Tanzania (1980)	86	14	70	8	6	—	9	—	6	—	1	—
Indonesia	88	12	8	80	1	1	2	—	3	—	2	1
Ethiopia	89	11	76	—	13	—	3	—	8	—	—	—
Mexico	90	10	8	81	—	1	1	—	4	—	4	1
Saudi Arabia	96	4	—	96	—	—	—	—	3	—	1	—
Nigeria (1977)	99	1	5	93	1	—	—	—	—	—	—	1

Source: United Nations, *Yearbook of International Trade Statistics* (various years).

Table 4.2 The imports of nineteen selected countries in percentages of total value (most for 1981)

	1–3 (mainly primary products)	4–5 (mainly secondary products)	1 Food	2 Industrial supplies	3 Fuel	4 Machinery and equipment	5 Consumer goods	6 GNP[1] 1982
Japan	88	12	11	27	50	7	5	9,890
Czechoslovakia (1977)	55	45	9	31	15	40	5	5,820
USA	55	45	7	21	27	17	55	11,360
UK	56	44	12	31	13	30	14	7,920
Bangladesh (1978)	77	23	20	43	14	19	4	120
Canada	38	62	7	21	10	50	12	10,130
India	85	15	9	32	44	14	1	240
Brazil	80	20	8	19	53	18	2	2,050
New Zealand	56	44	6	34	16	34	10	7,090
Argentina	58	42	4	42	12	36	6	2,390
Peru	48	52	15	32	1	44	8	930
Australia	43	57	4	25	14	40	15	9,820
Venezuela	46	54	14	32	0	43	11	3,630
Tanzania (1980)	58	42	8	30	20	36	5	260
Indonesia	60	40	6	33	21	26	14	420
Ethiopia	57	43	8	25	24	34	9	140
Mexico	41	59	8	30	3	45	14	2,130
Saudi Arabia	40	60	11	29	0	41	19	11,260
Nigeria	41	59	13	28	1	47	11	1,010

Note: [1] Gross National Product per inhabitant.
Source: United Nations, *Yearbook of International Trade Statistics* (various years).

surprises. From general knowledge and with reference to other sources of information note the main products you would expect the developing countries on the list to export. Is foreign trade beneficial to the countries that trade. How necessary is it? Do you think that countries trade because there are products that they have to import? Or do they trade because there is an advantage in exporting some products rather than selling them all at home? What primary products are exported by the United Kingdom or the United States? You might have been surprised to find that manufactures make up a large proportion of the exports of some developing countries, including Bangladesh, India and Brazil. Could it be that Bangladesh and India do not have enough primary products to spare? China, too, is increasing its exports of manufactures. In contrast Australia, though in many respects highly developed, mainly exports primary products. The same is true of the Soviet Union.

With reference to table 4.2 it may be surprising that so many of the developing countries included are large importers of primary products. Some, like Bangladesh, Peru and Venezuela import large quantities of food and for some, particularly Brazil and India, fuel is the largest item of import in value.

You may appreciate better what is going on if you plot the following pairs of variables on graph paper:

1 Plot imports of manufactured goods (table 4.2) or secondary products, i.e. the sum of columns 4 + 5 against exports of manufactured goods (in table 4.1) or secondary products, i.e. the sum of columns 5–10. Both scales will be from 0 to 100 per cent.
2 Scale GNP per inhabitant down by 100 (i.e. move the decimal point two places to the left, then round). You can then plot GNP (horizontal axis) against the export of primary products in table 4.1. You should obtain a negative correlation if developing countries (as defined by GNP) are exporters of primary products.
3 Plot GNP against the export of secondary products.

Flows of international trade

The total picture of international trade is enormously complicated since any pair of countries from among some two hundred can trade in anything from half a dozen to thousands of different classes of products, depending how detailed you want to be: tinned pineapples, tropical fish, plywood, bismuth, copper wire. An appreciation of the major types of product entering world trade and the major flows is essential for an appreciation of the problems of the developing world. Fortunately the *United Nations Statistical Yearbook* provides an array of data that, although formidable, can be reduced to something just about comprehensible.

In tables 4.3–4.6 almost all the countries of the world have been allocated to twelve regions. You should read the notes that follow to be sure you are clear which countries make up each region. The first five and the last two are developed regions and the five intervening ones are developing.

When you are sure of the twelve regions, look at tables 4.3–4.6. Four classes of products entering world trade are studied: food, crude materials, fuel and just one sector of manufactured goods: machinery and transport equipment. Other sectors of industry not included are also important: 'chemicals' and 'other manufactured goods'. On a piece of paper mark each region as a box or node roughly where it is located in the world. Then from the data in each table join regions which exchange products. You will need a different diagram for each of the four types of trade. If you can work in a group, then the plotting can be shared. For simplicity you can simply plot net flows. For example, in table 4.6 the United States exports 4000 million dollars' worth of machinery to Japan but imports 21,000 million from Japan. Instead of drawing both flows you can find the difference (unless the flows are equal or too small to record) and put one flow only, in the example above 17,000 million from Japan to the United States.

You will find that on the whole the developing regions are still mostly net importers of manufactured goods, while the developed regions are mostly net exporters. Note also the large amount of trade within Western Europe (mostly trade within the European Economic Community). There is a large trade in manufactures between developed regions and a large export of primary products from Canada, the United States, Australia and the Soviet Union.

Finally try to reason out the following possibility. In the last century only a few countries exported manufactured goods, while many countries imported them. As more and more countries industrialize, will there not be a time when there will be many like those of Western Europe and Japan scouring the world for raw materials and fuel? Which countries will then have an advantage? Will Australia, the Soviet Union, Canada and the Middle East oil countries, among the richest in natural resources to population in the world, be dictating conditions in world trade?

Tables 4.3–4.6 World trade by commodity classes and regions

Notes: 1 Full regional definitions:
  WEU West Europe (all non-members of CMEA, including Yugoslavia)
  AUS Australia includes New Zealand
  AFR Africa excluding South Africa
  LAM Latin America
  MEA Middle East from Turkey to Yemen to Iran
  SAS South and South-east Asia from Afghanistan to Indonesia to Philippines
  CHI China and Mongolia, North Korea, Vietnam
  EEU East Europe excluding USSR and Yugoslavia

Table 4.3 World trade in food, thousands of millions of US dollars (blank = less than 50 million)

From \ To	WEU	CAN	USA	JAP	AUS	AFR	LAM	MEA	SAS	CHI	EEU	USR	Worl
WEU	55	1	3	1		6	2	4	1		2	2	78
CAN	1	–	2	1			1					1	7
USA	8	2	–	4		2	5	1	3	1	2	1	30
JAP				–					1				2
AUS	1		2	2				1	1	1		1	10
AFR	5		1			1						1	10
LAM	9		7	1		1	3	1			1	5	29
MEA	1							1					3
SAS	3		1	3		1		1	3			1	15
CHI									2	–	1		5
EEU	2					1		1			3	2	10
USR												–	1
World	89	3	17	13	1	12	12	12	13	6	22	14	210

Table 4.4 World trade in crude materials, thousands of millions of US dollars, 1980 (blank less than 500 million)

From \ To	WEU	CAN	USA	JAP	AUS	AFR	LAM	MEA	SAS	CHI	EEU	USR	Wor
WEU	28		1			1		1			2	1	35
CAN	4	–	5	2									12
USA	9	2	–	5		1	2		3	1			29
JAP				–					1				2
AUS	2			2					1				6
AFR	4												7
LAM	5		2	2		1					1		12
MEA	1												2
SAS	4		2	5					5	1	1		19
CHI	1			1						–	1		3
EEU	2			1							5		11
USR	2										4	–	8
World	64	2	10	19	1	4	5	3	12	4	11	3	13

2 AFR, LAM, MEA, SAS and CHI are defined as developing.
3 For simplicity South Africa and some small Pacific countries are excluded.
4 Values are rounded and as a result of omissions and rounding row and column values do not add up to world total.
5 Within region trade is possible where more than one country is involved but not in the cases of single countries Canada (CAN), USA, Japan (JAP), China (CHI), USSR (USR).

Source: United Nations, *Statistical Yearbook* (1981), table 179.

Table 4.5 World trade in mineral fuels, thousands of millions of US dollars, 1980 (blank = less than 500 million)

From \ To	WEU	CAN	USA	JAP	AUS	AFR	LAM	MEA	SAS	CHI	EEU	USR	World
WEU	55		2			2	1	1					66
CAN		–	8	1									9
USA	3	2	–	2			1						8
JAP				–									1
AUS				1									2
AFR	32		27	1		1	6	1	1		2		71
LAM	6	2	24	1		1	11						46
MEA	80	2	20	42	3	3	12	7	25		2	1	198
SAS			5	14			1		7				29
CHI				2						–			3
EEU	4										2		42
USR	19					1			1		13	–	36
World	201	6	86	64	4	8	33	10	35	1	19	1	477

Table 4.6 World trade in machinery and transport equipment, thousands of millions of US dollars (blank = less than 500 million)

From \ To	WEU	CAN	USA	JAP	AUS	AFR	LAM	MEA	SAS	CHI	EEU	USR	World
WEU	155	2	19	2	3	21	12	18	11	2	6	5	261
CAN	1	–	13				1						16
USA	24	18	–	4	3	2	16	6	9		1		86
JAP	12	1	21	–	2	4	5	7	14	2		1	71
AUS													1
AFR													
LAM	1		1				3						5
MEA							1						2
SAS	3		7	1		1	1	1	5				20
CHI										–			1
EEU	2					1	1	1	1	1	17	16	46
USR	1					1	1	1	1	1	7	–	12
World	199	22	61	8	9	32	40	35	40	7	46	22	511

Case study E

A multinational company: Shell

Shell Transport and Trading (not the same as its associated company Royal Dutch Shell) is a multinational or transnational company.
What does Shell Transport and Trading (STT) do?

agriculture	natural gas
chemicals	oil and gas exploration
coal	oil production
forestry	pipeline
manufacturing – oil	research
marketing	services
marine	storage
metals	

(Royal Dutch Shell does most of the exploring and extracting of oil.)

Who owns STT and Royal Dutch? The shareholders (none apparently in developing countries) are distributed as shown in table E.1.

Table E.1

Shareholders	Royal Dutch 500,000 (%)	STT 340,000 (%)	Combined (%)
UK	5	98	42
USA	33	1	20
Netherlands	29	< 1	17
Switzerland	20	< 1	12
France	8	1	5
German FR	3	< 1	2
Belgium	1	< 1	1

Where does STT operate? The answer is in table E.2 where the number of operating units is given for each country. Shell operates many of the units listed jointly with other companies. Refer to a good-sized political map of the world and find the various countries listed. Which important countries are not on the list?

How much is Shell worth? On 12 August 1985 (*The Times* gives the capitalization of the main British-based companies every Monday): STT

Case study E (*continued*)

Table E.2 Operating companies – group and associated of Shell TT

Developed		*Asia*		*South America*		*Africa (contd.)*	
Austria	3	Abu Dhabi	3	Argentina	2	Guinea	1
Belgium	4	Bangladesh	1	Brazil	4	Ivory Coast	3
Denmark	3	Brunei	4	Chile	1	Kenya	4
Finland	2	China	2	Colombia	3	Lesotho	1
France	11	Cyprus	1	Ecuador	1	Libya	1
Gibraltar	1	Hong Kong	2	Paraguay	1	Malawi	1
Greece	2	India	1	Peru	2	Mali	2
Ireland	6	Indonesia	8	Surinam	2	Mauritius	1
Italy	1	Laos	1	Uruguay	1	Morocco	1
Luxembourg	1	Malaysia	7	Venezuela	1	Mozambique	1
Netherlands	18	Oman	2			Niger	1
Norway	1	Pakistan	1	*Africa*		Nigeria	2
Portugal	2	Philippines	7			Reunion	1
Spain	5	Qatar	2	Algeria	1	Senegal	2
Sweden	1	Saudi Arabia	2	Angola	1	Sierra Leone	2
Switzerland	2	Singapore	3	Botswana	1	Somalia	1
UK	14	South Korea	3	Burkina Faso[1]	1	South Africa	3
West Germany	8	Syria	1	Cameroon	1	Swaziland	1
		Thailand	7	Cape Verde	1	Tanzania	2
Australia	12	Turkey	3	Central Africa	1	Togo	1
New Zealand	6			Chad	1	Tunisia	4
		Middle America		Djibouti	1	Uganda	1
Canada	5			Egypt	1	Zaire	2
USA	7	Caribbean	15	Ethiopia	2	Zambia	1
		El Salvador	3	Gabon	1	Zimbabwe	2
Japan	11	Guatemala	2	Gambia	1		
		Honduras	1	Ghana	1		
		Mexico	1				
		Nicaragua	2				

Note: [1] formerly Upper Volta
Source: Shell Transport and Trading Company plc, *Annual Report 1984.*

£7562m. and Royal Dutch £11,802m. Is that a lot? Each year Shell's profits (i.e. revenue minus costs) are several hundred million pounds a year. Some of the profits go back in tax to host countries, some has to be reinvested, while shareholders get the residue. Who gains from this whole operation? Would the developing countries be able to run mines, industries, services, without transnational companies?

Development assistance

Foreign trade is widely regarded as beneficial to both or all partners in a particular set of transactions. Each country, in theory, is importing something from somewhere else more cheaply than it would cost to produce at home. The general idea of foreign trade is that there is a broad balance, the value of the imports and exports of each country being roughly equal.

What is called development assistance by the United Nations is different. Such assistance is found in various forms and it includes not only gifts from one country to another but also loans and investment. Gifts and loans, the latter especially if made with low rates of interest, are thought of as aid, but the term investment implies a return and perhaps the idea of profit and even of exploitation of developing by developed countries.

Three questions (among others) must be asked about foreign assistance: how much of what should be given to which countries? Money perhaps comes to mind first, but money is really only a credit of so much to obtain some goods or services. To help a developing low-income country you could send consumer goods such as clothing, blankets or food. On the other hand you could send equipment or fertilizers to help increase productive capacity in industry or agriculture. Which kind of transfer do you think would be more useful in the end? It would also be possible to move people from areas that were lacking in agricultural land and mineral resources to better endowed areas. What problems might arise here?

Case study F

From *Mankind at the Turning Point*
M. Mesarovic and E. Pestel

Many recent analyses of the long-term prospects for mankind have produced gloomy conclusions. Promptly, they were called doomsday prophecies. Yet the rapid succession of crises which are currently engulfing the entire globe are the clearest indication that humanity is at a turning point in its historical evolution. And the way to make doomsday prophecies self-fulfilling is to ignore the obvious signs of perils that lie ahead – which indeed are already felt – and rely solely on 'faith.' *Our scientifically conducted analysis of the long-term world development based on all available data points out quite clearly that such a passive course leads*

Case study F (*continued*)

> *to disaster*. It is *most urgent* that we do not avert our eyes from the dangers ahead, but face the challenge squarely and assess alternative paths of development in a positive and hopeful spirit. Starting early enough on a new path of development can save mankind from traumatic experiences if not from catastrophes. The concept of the 'organic growth' of mankind, as we have proposed in this report, is intended as a contribution toward achieving that end. Were mankind to embark on a path of organic growth, the world would emerge as a system of interdependent and harmonious parts, each making its own unique contribution, be it in economics, resources, or culture.
>
> The concept of the organic growth of the world system is not to be construed as a simplistic one-world 'monolithic' concept of world development; indeed a homogeneous one-world concept is essentially incompatible with a truly global approach to better the predicament of mankind. Such an approach must start from and preserve the world's regional diversity. Paths of development, region-specific rather than based on narrow national interests, must be designed to lead to a sustainable balance between the interdependent world-regions and to global harmony – that is, to mankind's growth as an 'organic entity' from its present barely embryonic state. (pp. vii–viii).

Are the high-income countries obliged to send assistance to low-income countries? Not at all, since international law does not require such transfers. There is no world government. To what extent are high-income countries committed to send assistance? Not to any great extent, although it was accepted some years ago that countries should provide not less than 0.7 per cent of their yearly GNP. Is that a great sacrifice? Is it enough to make much impact on the developing world? Should it be spread evenly over the developing countries according to population or concentrated in certain regions? If concentrated, should it go mainly to the very low-income countries, to places where it can bring the most benefit?

The data in tables 4.7 and 4.8 should convince you that most rich countries are not over generous. Of the seventeen countries of the Organization for Economic Co-operation and Development (OECD), only five (see column 3) provided more than 0.7 per cent of their GNP in 1983. In that same year only two countries of the Organization of Petroleum Exporting Countries (OPEC) did, though several more had been more

Table 4.7   Official development assistance from OECD (1983), OPEC (1983) and CMEA (1977) members

OECD	1983 1	2	3	OPEC	1983 1	2	3	1975 4
			%				%	%
Netherlands	1,268	88	1.02	Kuwait	995	622	4.46	7.18
Norway	526	128	0.99	Saudi Arabia	3,916	377	3.53	7.76
Denmark	449	88	0.85	United Arab Emirates	100	71	0.42	11.68
Sweden	737	89	0.80	Qatar	22	73	0.42	15.58
France	3,790	69	0.77	Libya	85	26	0.35	2.29
Belgium	410	41	0.59	Venezuela	141	8	0.20	0.11
Canada	1,535	62	0.47	Iran	139	3	0.13	1.12
German FR	2,767	45	0.45	Algeria	44	2	0.09	0.28
Australia	773	51	0.45	Nigeria	35	0.4	0.05	0.04
Finland	178	37	0.36	Iraq	−3	−	−	1.62
Japan	4,319	36	0.35					
UK	1,432	26	0.33				1977	
Italy	1,105	20	0.32	CMEA		2		
Switzerland	286	44	0.30					
New Zealand	59	18	0.28	Romania		12		
Austria	181	24	0.28	USSR		11		
USA	8,698	37	0.23	Hungary		10		
				German DR		5		
				Czechoslovakia		4		
				Poland		3		
				China		0.2		

Key: 1   Total in millions of US dollars
   2   US dollars transferred per inhabitant of donor country
   3   Official development assistance as a proportion of total GNP of donor country
   4   As 3 but for 1975
Sources: World Bank, *World Development Report* (1985), table 18, and United Nations, *Statistical Yearbook* (1978), table 204, for CMEA.

forthcoming with funds in 1975 (why was that so?). It is difficult to work out comparable figures for the rich countries of the Council for Mutual Economic Assistance (CMEA, formerly COMECON), but none provided more than 0.7 per cent of its GNP in 1977. For the last few years the United Nations has not published any data at all for them.

Another way of looking at the generosity of donor countries is to express the aid they gave in dollars per inhabitant (see column 2 in table 4.7). These figures do not correlate exactly with the percentage of GNP in column 1 because the GNP per inhabitant varies greatly among the OECD countries. Kuwait and Saudi Arabia were particularly forthcoming with assistance and, among OECD members, the Netherlands and Scandinavia head the list. But why should France be so much more generous than the United Kingdom or

Table 4.8 Development assistance received by selected countries, average annual amount in US dollars per inhabitant, 1978–80

French Guiana	1,348	Egypt	39
Martinique	1,111	Burundi	23
New Caledonia	1,024	Bangladesh	13
Reunion	811	Thailand	11
St Helena	807	Philippines	10
Tuvalu	394	Pakistan	9
Seychelles	361	Nepal	9
Israel	263	Indonesia	7
Netherlands Antilles	258	Mexico	7
Surinam	201	Vietnam	6
Belize	140	Afghanistan	5
Botswana	124	Ethiopia	5
Djibouti	101	India	3
Fiji	68	Nigeria	1

Source: United Nations, *Statistical Yearbook* (1981), table 75.

Italy? Is it philanthropy or self-interest? So where does the assistance end up? To trace all the transfers from every donor country to every recipient of assistance would be a nightmare task.

Soviet sources show that, as might be expected, much of the assistance from the Soviet Union and its CMEA partners goes to countries defined as 'socialist'. The Korean DPR (North Korea), Mongolia, Vietnam and Cuba are close allies of the Soviet bloc, while Angola and Ethiopia have also received some assistance. In the past three decades much Soviet assistance has also been directed to Egypt, Syria, Iraq and India. Nicaragua has recently appeared on the Soviet trade and assistance 'map'. China received virtually none after 1960. It would be an over-simplification to imply that all CMEA assistance is political, ideological or strategic, but there is no doubt a strong element of each of these motives.

Western assistance is much greater in quantity than that from the Soviet Union and its CMEA partners and more widely distributed. Some is distributed through international agencies such as the World Bank and this part is less likely to be biased in destination towards developing countries regarded as sympathetic. Much aid is bilateral (i.e. from one donor to one recipient). The policy of Sweden is to give assistance where needed, rather than with conditions. France, on the other hand, tends to favour its former and present colonies, and the United Kingdom favours countries of the British Commonwealth. The United States, especially with its military aid, favours countries such as Israel and the Republic of Korea (South Korea), places of key strategic significance.

As a result of the various motives and influences at work in the distribution of development assistance there is no obvious pattern or consistency. The data in table 4.8 tell something. The aid received by India in 1978–80 was equivalent to US$3 per person each year. Each citizen of French Guiana got the equivalent of US$1350. The secret? There were about 700 million people in India, but in French Guiana a mere 70,000. To provide every Indian with US$1350 dollars in a year it would be necessary to transfer to India alone about 15 per cent of the whole GNP of the OECD countries. That reminds me of the calculation made by some Brazilian economists: if all the development assistance from all the developed countries in the world were channelled only to Brazil, then the Brazilian economy could become developed quite quickly. Brazil has less than 4 per cent of the population of all the developing countries. Does this imply that twenty-five times as much assistance is needed as is provided at present? Roughly perhaps, if not exactly, but to make a serious impact the transfer of perhaps 7 per cent of the GNP of the rich countries is nearer the mark than the elusive 0.7 per cent agreed on but not reached. And the assistance would have to be placed wisely (effectively – dare one say profitably?). More importantly, many people are worried that foreign assistance may upset traditional cultures and economies with the result that positive features would be lost in the drive to change techniques and raise productivity.

You should study the great disparities shown in table 4.8. You might like to sort the countries out according to US dollars of assistance received per inhabitant, the full definition being rather long-winded but useful to know: 'disbursements to individual developing countries or areas of bilateral official development assistance from developed market economies (e.g. France, Australia) and disbursements from multilateral institutions'. Why are some countries loved and others ignored? Is it size (Martinique), strategic position (Djibouti), possession of a valuable natural resource (New Caledonia), or just low income?

Key ideas

1 In most developing countries the value of total trade or imports to GNP is usually very high (with some noteworthy exceptions).
2 Developing countries tend to be net importers and the developed countries net exporters of manufactured goods.
3 Only a very limited amount of development assistance is given by the developed to the developing countries.

5
Problems and prospects for the Third World

Issues and authorities

In chapter 1 seven ingredients were given as convenient headings into which the world economy would be divided for the purposes of this book. Three (ingredients 2–4) were discussed in chapters 2 and 3: natural resources, means of production and products. The fifth, international transactions, was dealt with in chapter 4. In this last chapter special reference will be made to the way countries are organized (ingredient 7) and to policies affecting population (ingredient 1).

It is widely accepted that materially the inhabitants of some countries are much better off than the inhabitants of other countries. There is much evidence to support the view that, if anything, the gap in living standards between rich and poor countries has tended to widen in the last few decades. There is less agreement about the causes of what has been called the development gap and about how it might be narrowed in the future. Indeed not everyone is agreed that it should be narrowed, let alone closed, even if that were possible. A world forced to adopt life-styles and living standards like those, say, in Western Europe or the Soviet Union, would have lost much of the rich diversity that it still has. An appreciation of the above problems of Third World development requires some knowledge of different cultural, political and ideological viewpoints.

The initial pressure for development in other parts of the world, mainly implying increasing consumption of goods and services, has come from Europe and then also from other industrial regions, especially the United

States and Japan, for more than two hundred years. Some of the thinking behind ideological systems and political decisions in the developed countries will now be considered. Such systems have been transferred through colonial administrators and businesses, especially large transnational companies in recent decades, to the countries that now make up the Third World. The political and religious views of people in developing countries must also be considered for it is their way of life – basic like that of many communities in the tropical forests of the world, or sophisticated like that in India and China – that is being changed. Like many people, I have my own views about the world, and it is very difficult for me to be impartial in choosing what to write, in a very short space, on ideologies. For simplicity I shall identify a number of 'authorities' and a number of 'issues'. I have chosen these two terms because they are not particularly controversial. By authority I mean a person or a movement that has gained influence on the minds of many people.

For simplicity we often attribute an idea or a set of ideas to a particular person. In practice what we know about an individual nearly always comes from the interpretation of others. We do not have the time or the professional background to read and understand the Christian Bible and the works of Adam Smith, Thomas Malthus, Karl Marx, Charles Darwin and numerous others. Yet Europeans of the late twentieth century live in a society pervaded by ideas of, or ideas attributed to, such people, and to movements associated with them. Can we distil some of the very basic points made by them on issues of relevance to Third World Development?

I have concentrated mainly on the viewpoints worked out by people living before the twentieth century. Some 'successful' ideas, from the nineteenth century and earlier, those followed and accepted by many people, like the fittest species that have survived through time, still dominate our thinking. Only in the twenty-first century will it be possible to judge which ideas of the twentieth century will survive for a long time.

If you are interested in sorting out your views of the world, beware. Everyone will tell you that their view is the best, the only possible one, the true approach. Fortunately we in the West are more free than people in many countries to gain access to information about many different views. Beware also of people who hold mutually exclusive views.

Now refer to table 5.1. It is an attempt to recapitulate some of the points made in this book with regard to the important matter of viewpoints and attitudes. It can be expanded and, no doubt, improved. What do various authorities have to say about major issues?

These matters could be discussed either from the viewpoint of each authority by working along each row in turn, or by issues, column by column. What follows is something of a mixture. Only the surface is being scratched because there are many other authorities and many more issues.

Table 5.1 Authorities on issues

Issue Authority	Life after death	Helping the poor	Equal society	Nature	Availability of natural resources	Animal rights
Old Testament	Yes	Yes	Not necessarily	None	God provides	None
Modern Christian	Yes	Yes	No	Little	Some concern	Little
Marx himself	No	Remove causes of poverty			Little concern Capitalist	
Modern Marxist	No	Remove causes of poverty	Yes inevitable	Little	problem	None
Darwin	Not concerned	{ To a minimum level { To a minimum level			Adapt to limits	
Market economy	Does not care	Up to a point	Impossible	No	Little concern	No
Conservationist			Eventually	Must help	Great concern	Concern
Pure scientist	Needs evidence	Not concerned	Not concerned	To be investigated	We can find more	Experiments on animals

Other possible issues to consider: women's rights, minority rights, property rights.

The Christian Bible, interpreted in various ways for nearly two thousand years, has served at least three distinct functions. Firstly, it has provided an explanation for the creation of the world, an account now discredited through findings of scientists. Secondly, it provides a code of conduct for all those who have faith in Christianity, offering a path to a good position in the 'next life'. Thirdly, one of the guidelines of the Christian faith, the need to help the poor, is a major aspect of the work of the churches. Only this last aspect of Christianity seems to have much direct influence currently on problems of the Third World.

In spite of concern over the next life, Christian communities have often done well for themselves materially in this life, as many religious orders did in Europe in the Middle Ages by their knowledge and application of techniques to the use of natural resources and to methods of production. From the sixteenth to the nineteenth century a prime concern of the Christians who accompanied the explorers, conquerors and settlers of other lands was to convert the 'natives' to their religion. In the twentieth century emphasis has shifted. Many people working in or for the Church have tried to help the poor. Men and women of religion in such diverse places as north-east Brazil, southern Africa, Calcutta and the inner-city areas of Britain have pressed for greater help for the poor, deprived and underprivileged. Usually the funds available for distribution by Christian agencies helping in their own countries or in the developing countries are much smaller than those available to governments for the same purpose. The welfare state is based primarily on the contributions (often reluctant) of the taxpayers, not on the modest donations of some of the public to religious charities.

Ideas attributed to Thomas Malthus regarding population and natural resources may be noted at this stage because Malthus was himself a man of religion, a parson. He is credited with pointing out something that had long been known but perhaps not spelt out very clearly. A population, whether of animals or of humans, can grow at a geometrical rate, but the means of subsistence, in the time of Malthus mainly productive land, can only be extended more slowly. According to Malthus, we humans should exercise restraint and limit the size of our families. In his time sophisticated easy means of artificial contraception were not widely available. Infanticide was quite widely practised in Europe and death from starvation not uncommon. His message, not fully appreciated, was that, as good Christians, people should abstain in their sexual relations in order that population should not outgrow available natural resources.

The ideas of Charles Darwin on evolution and associated features of life on our planet, more than any other development perhaps, threatened the biblical description of the creation of the world as the home of man. Some of the ideas of Darwin seem to have indirectly affected our ideas about Third World Development.

Darwin was a natural scientist with interests in geology and biology. He was concerned particularly about the way present plants and animals had evolved, assuming they had not all been designed in blueprint form by God before the world was created. Professor J. M. Thoday of the University of Cambridge (*The Times*, 12 December 1981) puts the contemporary discussions of evolution in perspective.

1   The theory of evolution proper states that the diversity of living forms arose through modification by descent, most if not all forms having originated from common ancestors.
2   Evolution came through changes in individuals that could lead to some individuals having a better chance of survival than others or 'survival of the fittest'. The idea has been transferred by analogy to human societies.
3   Did evolution proceed smoothly or did sudden catastrophic changes occur and result in quick changes at certain times?

One of the ideas attributed to or at least clarified by Darwin, the idea of the survival of the fittest (species), seems to be compatible with the market economy in which the more profitable efficient producers thrive and the unprofitable inefficient ones go out of business. Adam Smith is seen by some as an early champion of free enterprise, with minimal state interference in economic affairs. Another idea of Darwin, evolution, seems compatible with ideas of Karl Marx about an inevitable path through various stages of economic and social organization of society from slave and feudal through capitalist to socialist and communist.

In his book *The Wealth of Nations*, published in 1776, Adam Smith wrote a great deal on the economy of the world. He noted that what we might now call expansion of the economy was taking place in some parts of the world, especially in the areas of English settlement in North America, but less in Britain. China was stagnating, while conditions were deteriorating in Bengal (now Bangladesh and the state of Bengal in India). Evidently there was a development gap then, though the term development itself was not used. The main idea attributed to Adam Smith is that the state, whether through national, or presumably also local, government, should not intervene excessively in economic affairs. The 'market' could function best if left alone to individuals, each to produce and exchange without restraint. The market economy goes back a long way, with its strong element of private ownership of means of production and private enterprise. Adam Smith also appreciated the significance of the application of new techniques in the Industrial Revolution.

In the publications of the United Nations the term 'market economy' is used with reference to developed and developing countries alike if there is a large private sector. Virtually all such countries now have some state influence and public ownership and strictly therefore they are 'mixed' economies. Some might say they are also mixed up. In the early 1980s political parties and leaders in the United States, the United Kingdom, and China, among others, have emphasized that competition is healthy. Private companies that make a loss should go out of business and should not be helped with public funds. By analogy, countries that are poor should not necessarily be assisted, because they are not making the effort they should.

Perhaps the most controversial and difficult of the authorities to interpret is Karl Marx. Marx carefully studies the economy of Europe, particularly that of Britain, around the middle of the nineteenth century. His writings show meticulous research in the collection of evidence to support his ideas, and some appreciation of the world economy as a whole. As well as being an economic historian, he was also up to a point ready to help to bring about change that he thought necessary in Europe, both as a thinker and a man of action.

One of the contributions of Marx to our thinking about development today was his idea that there are stages of economic and social development. Put in the most simple way possible, they are as follows. I have taken the liberty of simplifying the stages greatly.

1   Traditional societies with very low levels of production and minimal technology. Everyone is equally 'poor' materially.
2   Slave. Here some members of society work for others and on the whole get a poorer deal materially as well as having no freedom. Slavery was common in ancient Greece and Rome and was widespread again in the European colonies of the Americas well into the last century (ending in the United States with the Civil War, 1861–5). Most slaves worked as labourers in farms or mines or did domestic jobs.
3   Feudal. Here again the majority of the population served the minority, having a particular relationship that was not, however, as close as slavery. The land was the main source of wealth. Feudalism was the type of society identified by Marx as existing in the Middle Ages in Europe and broadly in Russia until the serfs were 'freed' in 1861.
4   Capitalist (actually there are several substages). Marx was living right in the middle of the period when industrial changes were coming fast in Britain and other parts of Europe. Here was a society in which mines and factories were now as important as sources of production as the land. A comparatively small number of industrialists, with buildings, machines, and transport links to the ends of the world, could control the economy and provide in return only minimum standards for the many workers. In a brief reference to the decline of local manufacturing in India at that time, Karl Marx saw the trend to be a step forward, eventually to be beneficial in forcing India into the factory age. Not everyone would see it as that today, though indeed modern India does

have some large industrial centres. This is as far as the stages had reached when Marx was thinking and writing. What happened after that is particularly significant for development in the future.

5   Instead of having wealth (the means of production) in a few hands under capitalism, it would be shared by the whole community under socialism and communism. It would be owned and controlled by the state or in collectives.

In the twentieth century the line of argument of Marx and his associates was followed by many people. One of the most influential was the Russian thinker, writer and politician, Lenin. It has largely fallen to the Communist Party of the Soviet Union to experiment with and put into practice Marxist ideas. The Soviet Union was the first socialist state in the modern world. Between the Revolution of 1917 and about 1930 almost all natural resources and means of production were taken over by the state in the Soviet Union. A revolution that theoretically, according to Marx, should have taken place in highly industrialized countries with large, oppressed, dissatisfied, urban workforces (the proletariat) took place instead in a predominantly rural country, which was only reaching the capitalist 'stage' in some regions.

The Soviet Union embarked in the 1920s on the correct (to a Marxist) inevitable path towards socialism (income varies according to job done), 'advanced' socialism and eventually communism (remunerate each according to his or her needs). By about 1930 virtually all means of production, including agricultural resources, were controlled by the state. Meanwhile the 'western' capitalist countries continued in their old ways, watering down the worst inequities with socialism of their own brand, but relentlessly exploiting their colonies and ex-colonies in Latin America, Africa and Asia. A late stage of capitalism, imperialism, was thought up by Marxists to describe this situation, many features of which have been discussed or will be discussed in this book and others in the series. The highly industrialized countries apparently needed the natural resources and markets of the rest of the world to prop up a doomed system at home.

Under the circumstances described above it is understandable that the Soviet Union should see itself as the champion of the developing world. It has helped to finance many development projects there, giving loans on favourable terms. It has no privately owned transnational companies, with their shareholders, to milk the poorer countries by making big profits out of economic activities conducted there.

Now we have got this far it is useful to take a Soviet view of the world and to note which countries are officially regarded as 'socialist' by the Soviet Union. The countries closest to the Soviet Union because they belong to the Council for Mutual Economic Assistance (CMEA) are the eight following, the last two being low-income countries: Bulgaria, Czechoslovakia, the German

DR, Hungary, Poland, Romania, Cuba, Mongolian People's Republic. Other countries recognized as 'socialist' are China, the Democratic People's Republic of Korea and Yugoslavia. Those known to have governments to which the Soviet Union is sympathetic and which may be 'Marxist' include Angola, Ethiopia, Kampuchea, Afghanistan and possibly Nicaragua, all five alluded to by President Reagan as areas with over much Soviet influence (Soviet 'client' states) before the summit conference in November 1985. Other countries that have received large amounts of Soviet aid at some stage in the period since 1945 include India, Iran, Iraq, Syria, Egypt, Algeria, Laos and Mozambique. Soviet leaders would no doubt like to see, and even help, more countries to follow the 'correct' predicted socialist path.

Marxist and neo-Marxist theorists and practising Soviet politicians and planners are not the only people who see stages of development and economic growth as inevitable. Reference was made earlier in this book to the assumption made in United Nations publications about such stages. The American economist and economic historian W. W. Rostow also put the case in his book *The Stages of Economic Growth: A non-Communist Manifesto*, referring to *The Communist Manifesto* of Marx of about a hundred years earlier.

Where do all these ideas lead us? You should now have some idea of the framework within which different groups of people may be thinking. Attitudes towards the developing countries may be influenced by them. The cavalier attitude towards nature, whether wild or domestic animals, or vegetation, may to some extent come from the idea expressed at various places in the Bible that the earth and all things on it were created (by God) for the use of man (and woman). The idea of instant creation 6000 years ago has limited acceptance now, even among practising Christians, but the ideas linger on. To Soviet Marxist-based planners and western transnational companies alike, the natural world is still something available to humans to be tamed and exploited indiscriminately. The developing countries are as much at risk in this game as the developed ones.

There are many other issues and views on them of relevance to Third World studies in addition to those in the table. Many people, especially, I suspect, people in rich countries, feel that too high material standards are bad and would bring problems to poor countries. Refer to case study G, pp. 82–3 for Geraldine Norman's attempt to measure 'gross national happiness' rather than GNP. People in rich countries themselves live in the comfort provided by an income of several thousand or more pounds or dollars a year. One of the simplest societies ever 'discovered' in the tropical forest is the tiny community of the Tasadays in the Philippines. Can such a society be preserved? Do its members want change? In Brazil the prospect for the Amazon Indians is elimination (deliberate or incidental), relegation to reservations or assimilation into the 'melting pot' with other Brazilians. Such simple societies are so fragile that they are at great risk. Many of the poor in the Third World do not aspire to ownership of a large house, a car, luxurious carpets and holidays abroad. They just want an adequate supply of clean water, a roof to keep out the rain, enough food and fuel to cook it with, some reliable medical support and some basic education, plus radios, some furniture, a bicycle. Can a compromise solution be reached?

Population

Here we return from the land of ideas and theories to the day-to-day problems of the world and take a final look at population, one of the most controversial matters in Third World development studies. Can we make any progress towards answering the very difficult question: how many people can (or should) the world support? We cannot hope to answer the question easily but it is the question behind many discussions on population in particular and development in general. One inescapable further question would have to be asked before the 'how many people?' question could be tackled: what standard of living should they have?

Since there is not just one government for the whole world but many, it is not the concern of anyone to work out how many people there should be. On the other hand, thought has been given in some countries to the number of people they should have in the future, as for example in the late 1970s in China. The Chinese ideas are of interest because China is so big that it is like a world in miniature. What is more, it has existed for a very long time as a cultural unit, with a civilization going back four thousand years or so. To look ahead for one hundred years is not difficult on that sort of time-scale.

By 1980 China's population had reached nearly 1000 million. There were already 10 people per hectare of cultivated land. The population would easily grow to 1500 million in two or three decades if the growth of population were to continue at the rate of the 1960s. Something had to be done. In their very long-term plan, Chinese planners recommended a population of 600–700 million people (still large) by the year 2080. The country would then be much more highly industrialized than now, and agricultural production would be three times as big as now. But what was the limit given for the total number of people? *Water*. There would only be enough to provide an adequate supply for the expected needs of 700 million people. Even the grandchildren of the Chinese planners who worked out the figure of 700 million will be very old, if not already dead, by 2080. The plan is pure speculation, if not demographic fiction. We cannot know what will happen that far ahead in China. The important point, perhaps, is that actually to change the structure and stabilize the size of the population of a country you need many decades.

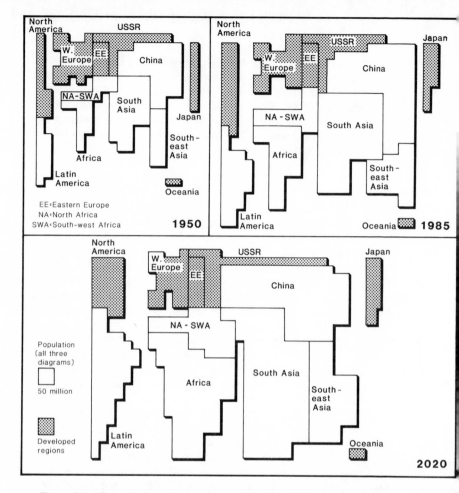

Figure 5.1 Growth of world population 1950–1985–2020 by major regions. Developed regions are shaded. Populations calculated from data provided in Population Reference Bureau, *World Population Data Sheet*, 1985. Japan includes the Republic of Korea (South), China includes Hong Kong, Taiwan and the Korean Republic (North) and East Europe includes Yugoslavia.

Some time ago a panel of experts estimated that the best or optimum population for the United Kingdom (56 million at present) would be about 30 million. In both Canada and Australia, two of the countries of the world most generously endowed with natural resources per inhabitant, concern has been expressed over the need to restrain further population growth as 'pressure' on land and natural resources grows. In many countries, both developed and developing, leaders and planners now see a need to reduce the rate of population growth, but there are exceptions. There was a story that the Mexicans (75 million in 1985) wanted to exceed in population their neighbour the United States (nearly 240 million in 1985) in order to be able to push the United States around. The President of the time had eight children. In the Soviet Union the Russian and other 'European' peoples are not growing fast and manpower is short in Siberia. Family planning is not encouraged.

To appreciate the population 'problem' in the world we must first examine trends and prospects and then consider whether or not population size should be controlled. Table 5.2 will be used as a beginning. Beware of differences in the yearly intervals. Work out from the data the average amount by which the population of the world increased, in millions, in each interval of 5, 10, 15 or 20 years. For example, it increased between 1920 and 1930 by 200 million, or by 20 million a year.

Table 5.2 The population of the world in millions in selected years since 1920

1920	1,810	1970	3,700
1930	2,010	1975	4,070
1940	2,250	1980	4,430
1950	2,525	1985	4,850
1955	2,760	2000	6,140
1960	3,040	2020	7,760
1965	3,350		

Sources: United Nations, *Demographic Yearbook* (1979), and Population Reference Bureau, *World Population Data Sheet* (1985) for 2000 and 2020.

The population of the world continues to increase rapidly and the Population Reference Bureau (in its 1985 *World Population Data Sheet*) estimates that if trends continue, even perhaps with some reduction in growth in most developing countries, there would be an increase of over 2900 million by the year 2020. Less than 200 million of the increase would be in the developed countries and over 2700 million in the developing (or less developed) ones, by today's definition of development.

You can now study the data in table 5.3 in order to find how the population of the world is distributed. Instead of the five continents (figure 5.1), or every country (the list would be too long) I have grouped the countries of the world into fourteen regions, seven largely developed, seven developing. It may be interesting to draw on a piece of graph paper squares or rectangles proportional in size to the population of each of the fourteen regions and then to look at an equal-area world map. Another exercise

Table 5.3 Demographic data for fourteen major regions of the world

	1 Total population	2 % urban	3 Birth-rate	4 Death-rate	5 Natural change	6 Infant mortality	7 Fertility	8 % under 15	9 % over 64
Australia and New Zealand	19	86	16	8	8	11	1.9	25	10
Canada	25	76	15	7	8	10	1.8	23	10
USA	236	74	16	9	7	11	1.8	22	12
USSR and MPR	276	64	20	10	10	32	2.5	25	10
Eastern Europe	134	57	16	11	5	22	2.1	23	12
Western Europe	357	75	13	10	3	13	1.8	21	14
Japan	120	76	13	6	7	7	1.7	23	9
Central America	133	59	32	6	26	57	4.6	42	4
South America	264	69	30	8	22	68	4.0	37	5
Africa south of Sahara	407	26	46	17	29	124	6.5	45	3
North Africa and South-west Asia	292	46	40	12	28	104	5.8	43	3
South Asia	978	23	36	14	22	128	5.2	41	3
South-east Asia including Taiwan	481	30	31	10	21	77	4.2	38	3
China	1,035	21	21	8	13	35	2.6	34	5
Less developed with China	3,596	32	32	11	21	94	4.4	38	4
Less developed without China	2,561	36	37	13	24	107	5.1	40	4
More developed	1,166	71	16	9	6	19	2.0	23	12
World	4,762	40	28	11	17	84	3.8	35	6

Key: 1 Total population in millions, mid-1984. Due to the omission of some small areas there are discrepancies between regional and grand totals.

2 Population defined as urban as a percentage of total population.

3, 4 Births and deaths per 1000 total population, early 1970s.

5 Annual rate of natural change per thousand.

6 Annual number of deaths of infants under the age of 1 per thousand live births.

7 Total fertility rate: average number of children that would be born to each woman if she produced in her childbearing lifetime at the same rate as women of those ages who actually did in a given year.

8, 9 Percentage of total population under 15 and over 64 years of age.

Source: Population Reference Bureau, *World Population Data Sheet* (1984).

could be to project the population of each region into the future using the current rates of change in column 5. You must move the decimal point one place to the left to get the annual percentage change.

Further work can be done with the data in table 5.3. You can make assumptions about possible changes in the rates of change themselves. What would cause them to change? Look at columns 6 and 7 in table 5.3. What would the effect be of an increase or a decrease in infant mortality rates, or in fertility? Has much international migration taken place in the 1980s? How drastic an effect do wars and famines have on population change?

Everyone would agree that there must be some limit to the number of people the world can contain, even if that time only comes when there is not enough space for them to lie down. Few people would feel competent to give even an approximate upward limit, though there is a feeling now that the population of the world might eventually level out at about 10,000 million. This situation would not arise until the twenty-second century, unless other developing regions of the world follow the example of China and introduce drastic controls on fertility rates. In China family planning has had dramatic effects already in the larger cities with one-child families very common. It has been much more difficult to organize family planning in the rural areas (see plates 5.1 and 5.2).

You should note that many of the thinkers among both Roman Catholics and Marxists, perhaps for different reasons, do not regard family planning as necessary or desirable in general terms. Large families are common also in many parts of Africa and Asia where neither Roman Catholicism nor Marxism has any influence.

Natural resources, production and population

In this section population will be related to natural resources and to production. Let us start with some major questions. Is the availability of natural resources ultimately the limit to the total amount of goods and services that can be produced in a given time (such as a year)? How big can the annual 'cake' be? How evenly is it being shared out though? Are the two questions related? Try working through the problem with the help of two sets of data in table 5.4.

Two sets of data are given in table 5.4 for the twenty largest countries of the world in population as well as for Canada and Australia. The values of GNP per inhabitant in column 1 are already familiar. Those for natural resources per inhabitant are not. They have been worked out as follows. As was done in chapter 2 of this book, an assessment was made of the bioclimatic and mineral resources of each country. Equal weight was given (arbitrarily) to the bioclimatic, fossil fuel and non-fuel mineral resources of each country. It was then possible to calculate what share (in percentages)

Plates 5.1 and 5.2   The population explosion in Ethiopia (1973) before the devastating famine of 1984–5. People are dressed in rags, standing here on over-used pasture land. Dung is widely used for fuel.

Table 5.4 Gross national product and natural resources per inhabitant

	GNP per person	Natural resource score*		GNP per person	Natural resource score*
China	290	30	Italy	6,350	30
India	260	30	Philippines	760	40
USSR	6,350	290	UK	9,050	50
USA	14,090	240	France	10,390	40
Indonesia	560	40	Thailand	810	70
Brazil	1,890	120	Turkey	1,230	50
Japan	10,100	15	Egypt	700	40
Bangladesh	130	15			
Pakistan	390	20	Canada	12,000	920
Nigeria	760	40	Australia	10,780	1280
Mexico	2,240	90			
German FR	11,420	60	World	2,760	100
Vietnam	250	15			

Note: * see text for explanation
Sources: GNP per person – Population Reference Bureau, *World Population Data Sheet* (1985); natural resource score – J.P. Cole, *Geography of World Affairs* (1983).

of the total of natural resource 'points' each country had. This was then divided by its share (also in percentages) of the total population of the world. Thus, for example, Australia had about 0.35 per cent of the population of the world but 4.5 per cent of all natural resources. The resulting score was 12.8. The average score for the whole world would (of course) be 1.00 because the world has 100 per cent of both population and natural resources. The data in column 2 of table 5.4 were calculated in the way described and then multiplied by 100 to remove decimal points.

On the basis of the calculations made, Canada has about 60 times as many natural resources per inhabitant as Japan, and Australia 85. Other calculations and weightings were made of the natural resources of each country but, however they are done, with reasonable care and common sense, Australia would come out with somewhere between 40 and 100 times as many as Japan.

On a piece of graph paper plot each country according to its position on the two variables GNP per inhabitant and natural resource score. Your vertical scale for GNP will have to be from 0 to 14,000 and, with the omission of Canada and Australia which would not fit on the sheet, the horizontal one for natural resources should go from 0 to 300.

When you have plotted the twenty countries, see if you can find any relationship between the two variables. Then think about the following points:

1   Where does a country move on the graph when more natural resources are found? What happens as natural resources are used up?
2   Where does a country move if its GNP rises or falls?
3   What happens as population grows?
4   How is international trade related to this graph?

You may wonder how you came to live in one of the countries perched rather far to the top left of the graph. Is that preferable to being at the lower left? Is GNP per inhabitant like a meter that measures the rate at which natural resources are used up? Japan, West Europe and also East Europe import large quantities of fuel and raw materials as well as some food. Where do these products come from? If the countries at the lower left were to become much more industrialized than they are now (they would go up the GNP per inhabitant scale), where would *they* get primary products?

Case study G

Measuring happiness

In an article in *The Times* of 26 May 1975, 'Introducing the hedonometer, a new way of assessing national performance *or* Why we should measure happiness instead of income', Geraldine Norman compares England and Botswana under six headings.

Three years ago I spent my honeymoon in the eastern highlands of Rhodesia trying to construct a hedonometer, a means of measuring happiness per head of the population. I did not have a thermometer type of thing in mind: it was to be a statistical structure, on the lines of Keynesian national accounting, that would end up by measuring gross national happiness instead of gross national product. The unit of measurement would be psychological satisfaction rather than money. I envisaged my hedonometer as a tool for political policy making of such power that boring chat about economic growth would be ousted, forgotten and interred.

The motivation for this eccentric undertaking was a growing conviction that the accretion of wealth and/or the expansion of income, whether at national or individual level, was not necessarily a recipe for happiness. Indeed, I suspected that in some cases greater wealth reduced the likelihood of happiness – that in certain circumstances there could be a negative correlation between happiness and money. . . .

Case study G (*continued*)

From my psychology book (C. J. Adcock's *Fundamentals of Psychology*) I learnt that the two primary needs of a human being are security and achievement, achievement being the positive satisfaction of individual and species drives. Conning his book with attention – and using a bit of imagination – I arrived at the six principal factors which contribute to a happy life, the basis of my hedonometer. The list is as follows (the first two factors provide security and the next four require satisfaction for an adequate level of achievement):

1   Understanding of your environment and how to control it.
2   Social support from family and friends.
3   Species drive satisfaction (sex and parental drives).
4   Satisfaction of drives contributing to physical well-being (hunger, sleep, etc.).
5   Satisfaction of aesthetic and sensory drives.
6   Satisfaction of the exploratory drive (creativity, discovery, etc.).

Table G.1

	Importance	England		Botswana	
		Satisfaction (%)	Product (score)	Satisfaction (%)	Product (score)
Understanding	15	50	750	70	1,050
Social support	20	40	800	80	1,600
Species satisfaction	10	70	700	70	700
Physical well-being	35	92	3,220	72	2,520
Aesthetic	5	40	200	60	300
Exploratory	15	30	450	60	900
Total	100		6,120		7,070

You might like to modify the table by changing the relative importance of different factors, the scores, the countries, even the factors themselves. On the purely subjective judgement of Geraldine Norman, Botswana is a 'happier' place than England. The measurement of happiness is indeed difficult and very subjective. The exercise is very worthwhile, however, because it shows how the conventional measures of development such as energy consumption and GNP per inhabitant are really very subjective too.

Is it realistic for mankind just to drift along in the hope that at least things cannot get worse in the future? Perhaps there is a need for drastic measures, with central planning of the world economy through a strong world government. Are we a species that has got out of control through being too clever? Should we be on different farms if the farms were as unevenly stocked with animals in relation to fodder production as the countries of the world are with people in relation to natural resources? If we are not careful, we may even destroy all the animals and plants on which we, as a species, graze like parasites.

You may think that some of the last outlandish ideas are too drastic and even unpalatable. Better think about them than ignore them, even if you reject them. There should be many changes and developments during your lifetimes, the next half century or so. As the world 'shrinks', with ever improving systems of transport and communications, you need to be informed about every part of it. The famous British geographer, Sir Halford Mackinder, made the following point in a paper published in 1904:

From the present time forth, in the post-Columbian age [refers to explorations at the time of Columbus] we shall . . . have to deal with a

Plate 5.3 A school under construction in Tanzania (1975). President Nyerere, himself a 'teacher', gave prominence to education. To provide facilities for both children and adults was an enormous undertaking.

closed political system, and none the less that it will be one of world-wide scope. Every explosion of social forces, instead of being dissipated in a surrounding circuit of unknown space and barbaric chaos, will be sharply re-echoed from the far side of the globe, and weak elements in the political and economic organism of the world will be shattered in consequence.

Case study H

Gulliver on colonialism

But I had another Reason which made me less forward to enlarge his Majesty's Dominions by my Discovery. To say the truth, I had conceived a few Scruples with relation to the Distributive Justice of Princes upon those Occasions. For instance, A Crew of Pirates are driven by a Storm they know not whither, at length a Boy discovers Land from the Top-mast, they go on Shore to Rob and Plunder; they see an harmless People, are entertained with Kindness, they give the Country a new Name, they take formal Possession of it for their King, they set up a rotten Plank or a Stone for a Memorial, they murder two or three Dozen of the Natives, bring away a Couple more by Force for a Sample, return home, and get their Pardon. Here commences a new Dominion acquired with a Title by *Divine Right*. Ships are sent with the first Opportunity, the Natives driven out or destroyed, their Princes tortured to discover their Gold; a free License given to all Acts of Inhumanity and Lust, the Earth reeking with the Blood of its Inhabitants: And this execrable Crew of Butchers employed in so pious an Expedition, is a *modern Colony* sent to convert and civilise an idolatrous and barbarous People.

But this Description, I confess, doth by no means affect the *British* Nation, who may be an Example to the whole World for their Wisdom, Care, and Justice in Planting Colonies; their liberal Endowments for the Advancement of Religion and Learning; their Choice of devout and able Pastors to propagate *Christianity*, their Caution in stocking their Provinces with People of sober Lives and Conversations from this the Mother Kingdom; their strict regard to the Distribution of Justice in supplying the Civil Administration through all their Colonies with Officers of the greatest Abilities, utter strangers to Corruption; and to crown all, by sending the most Vigilant and Virtuous Governors, who

Case study H (*continued*)

have no other Views than the Happiness of the People over whom they preside, and the Honour of the King their Master.

But, as those Countries which I have described do not appear to have a Desire of being conquered, and enslaved, murdered or driven out by Colonies, nor abound either in Gold, Silver, Sugar or Tobacco; I did humbly conceive they were by no means proper Objects of our Zeal, our Valour, or our Interest. However, if those whom it may concern, think fit to be of another Opinion, I am ready to depose, when I shall be lawfully called, That no *European* did ever visit these Countries before me. I mean, if the Inhabitants ought to be believed; unless a Dispute may arise about the two *Yahoos*, said to have been seen many Ages ago on a Mountain in *Houyhnhnm-land*, from whence the Opinion is, that the Race of those Brutes hath descended; and these, for anything I know, may have been *English*, which indeed I was apt to suspect from the Lineaments of their Posterity's Countenances, although very much defaced. But, how far that will go to make out a Title, I leave to the Learned in Colony-Law.

But as to the Formality of taking Possession in my Sovereign's Name, it never came once into my Thoughts; and if it had, yet as my Affairs then stood, I should perhaps in point of Prudence and Self-preservation, have put it off to a better Opportunity.

This extract from *Gulliver's Travels* was written two hundred and fifty years ago. Gulliver is justifying to his readers why he did not lay claim to the countries he visited on behalf of his sovereign. Did the next two hundred and fifty years prove Swift right?

Key ideas

1   Since written records began a number of different authorities have had different views on a number of aspects of 'development' and 'underdevelopment'.

2   Few people are prepared to state with certainty what the limit is to the number of people the world can contain.

3   Massive variations continue to exist in the national shares of the global annual 'cake'.

Appendix: Development data set for the hundred largest countries of the world in population in the mid-1980s

| | | 1 | 2 | 3 | 4 | 5 |
		Population	Area	Population change	% urban	Natural resource score
1	China	1,042	9,561	11	21	1
2	India	762	3,046	22	23	1
3	USSR	278	22,402	10	64	4
4	USA	239	9,363	7	74	4
5	Indonesia	168	1,492	22	22	1
6	Brazil	138	8,512	23	68	3
7	Japan	121	370	6	76	0
8	Bangladesh	102	143	28	15	0
9	Pakistan	99.2	80	27	29	0
10	Nigeria	91.2	924	31	28	1
11	Mexico	79.7	1,973	26	70	2
12	German FR	61.0	248	− 2	94	2
13	Vietnam	60.5	333	25	19	0
14	Italy	57.4	301	1	72	1
15	Philippines	56.8	300	25	37	1
16	UK	56.4	244	1	76	2
17	France	55.0	574	4	73	1
18	Thailand	52.7	514	19	17	2
19	Turkey	52.1	781	25	45	2
20	Egypt	48.3	1,000	27	44	1
21	Iran	45.1	1,648	30	50	4
22	Korean Republic	42.7	98	17	57	0
23	Spain	38.5	505	6	91	2
24	Poland	37.3	312	10	59	3
25	Burma	36.9	678	22	24	2
26	Ethiopia	36.0	1,184	21	15	2
27	Zaire	33.1	2,345	29	34	4
28	South Africa	32.5	1,223	21	56	4
29	Argentina	30.6	2,777	16	83	4
30	Colombia	29.4	1,138	21	67	2
31	Canada	25.4	9.976	8	76	6
32	Morocco	24.3	444	29	42	3
33	Yugoslavia	23.1	256	7	46	2
34	Romania	22.8	238	5	49	2
35	Algeria	22.2	2,382	33	52	4
36	Sudan	21.8	2,506	29	21	4
37	Tanzania	21.7	937	35	14	2
38	Kenya	20.2	583	41	16	2
39	Korean DPR	20.1	121	23	64	1
40	Peru	19.5	1,285	25	65	4

6	7	8	9	10	11
% not agricultural	Energy consumption	Telephones	Infant mortality	% literate	GNP
33	580	0	38	60	290
39	200	0	118	42	260
85	5,770	9	32	98	6,350
98	9,430	79	11	99	14,090
43	230	0	87	68	560
64	700	6	71	73	1,890
91	3,500	46	6	99	10,100
17	50	0	133	31	130
48	210	0	120	29	390
49	200	1	105	30	760
66	1,760	7	53	84	2,240
97	5,510	46	10	99	11,420
31	130	0	90	40	250
90	2,890	34	12	96	6,350
56	330	2	50	89	760
98	4,540	48	10	99	9,050
92	4,000	46	9	99	10,390
26	360	1	51	88	810
50	790	4	110	66	1,230
51	620	1	80	42	700
64	1,030	3	101	43	1,500
65	1,440	8	29	92	2,010
85	2,280	32	10	93	4,800
72	4,470	10	19	98	4,190
50	70	0	94	69	180
23	30	0	142	6	140
27	70	0	106	58	160
72	2,640	11	92	57	2,450
88	1,650	9	35	95	2,030
75	900	6	53	83	1,410
96	9,700	69	9	99	12,000
51	300	1	99	29	750
66	2,330	10	32	87	2,570
55	4,640	8	28	96	2,500
53	740	3	109	41	2,400
25	90	0	118	26	400
21	50	1	98	74	240
24	100	1	82	49	340
57	2,680	1	32	90	1,500
65	610	3	99	80	1,040

		1	*2*	*3*	*4*	*5*
						Natural
				Population	*%*	*resource*
		Population	*Area*	*change*	*urban*	*score*
41	Venezuela	17.3	912	27	76	4
42	Nepal	17.0	141	24	6	1
43	German DR	16.7	108	1	77	2
44	Sri Lanka	16.4	66	21	22	1
45	Australia	15.8	7,695	9	86	6
46	Malaysia	15.7	333	22	32	3
47	Czechoslovakia	15.5	128	3	74	2
48	Iraq	15.5	435	33	68	4
49	Uganda	14.7	236	35	14	1
50	Afghanistan	14.7	658	25	16	2
51	Netherlands	14.5	34	4	88	2
52	Ghana	14.3	239	32	40	1
53	Mozambique	13.9	783	28	13	2
54	Chile	12.0	757	18	83	5
55	Saudi Arabia	11.2	2,150	30	70	6
56	Hungary	10.7	93	− 2	54	2
57	Syria	10.6	185	39	47	1
58	Portugal	10.3	92	5	30	1
59	Greece	10.1	132	5	70	2
60	Ivory Coast	10.1	246	28	42	1
61	Cuba	10.1	115	11	70	2
62	Madagascar	10.0	587	28	22	2
63	Belgium	9.9	31	1	95	0
64	Cameroon	9.7	475	26	42	2
65	Bulgaria	8.9	111	2	65	2
66	Ecuador	8.9	284	27	45	4
67	Zimbabwe	8.6	391	35	24	3
68	Sweden	8.3	450	0	83	2
69	Guatemala	8.0	109	35	39	2
70	Angola	7.9	1,247	25	24	3
71	Mali	7.7	1,240	28	18	1
72	Austria	7.5	84	0	55	1
73	Tunisia	7.2	164	23	52	1
74	Malawi	7.1	118	32	12	1
75	Burkina Faso*	6.9	274	26	8	1
76	Zambia	6.8	753	33	43	3
77	Senegal	6.7	196	31	42	1
78	Switzerland	6.5	41	2	58	0
79	Niger	6.5	1,267	28	16	2
80	Somalia	6.5	638	26	34	1

Note: * formerly Upper Volta

6	7	8	9	10	11
% not agricultural	Energy consumption	Telephones	Infant mortality	% literate	GNP
84	3,140	6	39	81	4,100
8	10	0	144	19	170
91	7,390	19	11	99	7,300
48	120	1	34	79	330
95	7,160	49	10	100	10,780
55	980	5	29	69	1,870
91	6,240	21	16	99	5,610
62	680	2	72	50	2,500
21	20	0	94	48	220
23	60	0	205	15	150
95	5,830	51	8	99	9,910
52	120	1	107	49	320
39	100	0	110	28	250
83	910	5	24	93	1,870
42	3,030	5	103	16	12,180
86	3,840	12	19	98	5,000
54	990	3	57	54	1,680
76	1,330	14	20	81	2,190
65	2,060	29	15	90	3,970
22	290	1	122	40	720
79	1,430	4	17	95	1,500
19	70	0	67	34	290
97	5,340	37	11	99	9,160
21	480	0	117	51	800
70	5,590	14	17	95	4,400
57	710	3	70	79	1,430
43	610	3	70	71	740
96	4,960	80	7	99	12,400
47	220	2	62	51	1,120
44	120	1	149	3	800
15	30	0	137	13	150
92	3,710	40	12	99	9,210
62	610	3	85	57	1,290
18	50	1	165	36	210
21	30	0	149	11	180
35	390	1	101	69	580
27	200	1	141	22	440
95	3,480	73	8	99	16,390
14	50	0	140	5	240
22	100	0	143	5	250

		1	2	3	4	5
				Population	%	Natural resource
		Population	Area	change	urban	score
81	Rwanda	6.3	26	36	5	0
82	Dominican Republic	6.2	49	25	52	1
83	Kampuchea	6.2	181	21	16	1
84	Bolivia	6.2	1,099	27	46	4
85	Yemen Arab Republic	6.1	195	27	15	0
86	Guinea	6.1	246	24	22	1
87	Haiti	5.8	28	23	28	0
88	Hong Kong	5.5	1	10	92	0
89	Chad	5.2	1,284	21	22	1
90	Denmark	5.1	43	− 1	83	1
91	El Salvador	5.1	21	21	39	0
92	Finland	4.9	337	5	60	3
93	Burundi	4.6	28	27	7	0
94	Honduras	4.4	112	34	37	2
95	Norway	4.2	324	2	71	4
96	Israel	4.2	21	18	87	0
97	Benin	4.0	116	28	39	1
98	Libya	4.0	1,760	35	64	6
99	Laos	3.8	237	23	16	1
100	Sierra Leone	3.6	72	17	28	1

Key: 1 Population in millions, 1985 (excludes Taiwan).
2 Area in thousands of km².
3 Annual rate of population change in per thousands.
4 Urban population as a percentage of total population.
5 Natural resource score based on availability of bioclimatic, fossil fuel and non-fuel mineral resources per inhabitant. The score is simplified and telescoped as follows in relation to world average score, which equals 100: 0–24, 0; 25–49, 1; 50–99, 2; 100–199, 3; 200–399, 4; 400–799, 5; 800 and over, 6.
6 Economically active population *not* engaged in agriculture as a percentage of total economically active population.
7 Consumption of energy in kilograms of coal-equivalent per inhabitant.
8 Telephones in use per 100 inhabitants.
9 Deaths of infants under the age of 1 year as a percentage of all live births.
10 Population over an eligible age able to read as a percentage of all such population.
11 Gross national produce in US dollars per inhabitant (values estimated for socialist countries 1, 3, 13, 24, 34, 39, 43, 47, 56, 61, 65, 83, 99, and for some others).
Sources: Population Reference Bureau, *World Population Data Sheet* (1985), for 1, 3, 4, 9, 11; J. P. Cole, *Geography of World Affairs* (1983), for 5; Food and Agriculture Organization, *Production Yearbook* (1983), for 6, table 3; United Nations, *Statistical Yearbook* (1981), for 7 and 8, table 188 for telephones; and Population Reference Bureau, *World's Children Data Sheet* (1982), for 10.

6	7	8	9	10	11
% not agricultural	Energy consumption	Telephones	Infant mortality	% literate	GNP
12	20	0	110	50	270
45	400	3	64	74	1,380
28	10	0	160	36	150
52	430	1	124	68	510
26	120	0	154	8	510
21	80	0	147	9	300
36	50	1	108	28	320
98	1,690	33	10	84	6,000
19	20	0	143	6	110
94	4,650	64	8	99	11,490
51	210	2	42	66	710
89	4,640	50	6	100	10,440
18	20	0	137	23	240
39	240	1	82	63	670
93	6,100	45	8	99	13,820
94	2,460	29	14	88	5,360
55	40	1	149	25	290
88	2,510	3	92	56	7,500
28	60	0	122	41	200
37	90	0	200	7	380

Discussion questions

Chapter 1

1 There are big disparities in living standards between countries. Should they be changed? If so, can they be changed?
2 What influence does each of the following have on the living standards of a country?

> Size of country (area, population, natural resources, GNP).
> Location of country in world (central – Egypt, peripheral – New Zealand, landlocked – Burundi).
> Natural resources in relation to population.
> Technology, mechanization, industry.
> Political, ideological system.

3 Refer to the data for energy consumption per inhabitant in table A and to the graph in figure A.

> 1 Pretend it is 1970 and cover up the graph after 1970. What would you say about the energy gap between 1937 and 1970?
> 2 In 1985 what would you say about the gap?
> 3 Put a piece of tracing paper on the graph and continue the consumption levels for the countries (a) as if the low-level consumers catch up with the high-level consumers; (b) as if the gap continues to exist; (c) as if the high-level consumers converge *downwards* with the low-level consumers. At what date do they converge according to your estimates?

Table A Energy consumption in kilograms of coal-equivalent per inhabitant

	China	India	Nigeria	Brazil	Japan	UK	USA
1937	NA	60	20	100	700	3,800	5,700
1950	50	70	30	180	510	3,740	7,470
1955	150	90	30	240	770	4,200	7,600
1960	450	110	30	310	1,030	4,280	8,050
1965	350	130	40	360	1,780	4,550	9,000
1970	350	140	50	440	3,250	4,870	10,810
1975	470	160	80	660	3,540	4,820	10,470
1980	570	180	140	770	3,670	4,800	10,420
1985*	650	220	200	850	3,500	4,500	9,000

Key: NA = not available.
Note: * estimate
Energy in coal-equivalent has been retrospectively scaled down from data in energy data sets in earlier years. Some of the values in this table have been interpolated by the present author.
Source: United Nations, *Energy Statistics Yearbook* (1982), table 1.

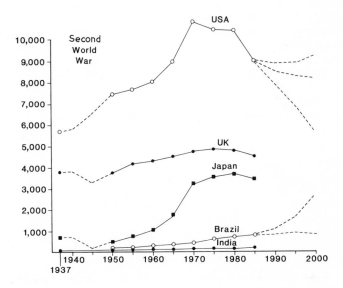

Figure A Energy consumption since the Second World War.

Chapter 2

1   Sort out your own views now as to which natural resources are renewable and which non-renewable.
2   The developed countries use up far more natural resources per inhabitant than the developing countries. How can this situation be changed?
3   Investigate sources of energy that are renewable (or better, inexhaustible).
4   How long can the natural environment sustain the attacks of the cultivators who plough excessively, the fishermen who over-fish, the loggers and gatherers of wood who never plant new trees? Conservationists are greatly concerned. Should you be?
5   If the population of the world suddenly stopped growing and stabilized, would that solve the problem?

Chapter 4

1   Is foreign trade advantageous to developing countries or would they do better to try to be self-sufficient? Is foreign trade beneficial to both parties in a particular trading transaction, as implied in the Brandt Report and its sequel?
2   Is enough aid being given really to help the developing countries? Cole (1981) in *The Development Gap* estimated that, to level out living standards in the world quickly, the United States would have to transfer about 80 per cent of its GNP elsewhere, Europe about 70 per cent. Would you like to think of our standard of living dropping by that much? Would such big transfers be physically possible anyway (sufficient ships and transport, ports in the right places, suitable products, services that could be adapted)? Cole implied that, very roughly, foreign official assistance at about 0.5 per cent of the GNP of the rich countries is not just one-tenth of what is needed but more like one-hundredth. Private aid (Oxfam spent £25 million in 1984) is about one-thousandth of what is needed.
3   Of the fossil fuels oil is the one most widely found in developing countries but it is also the one with the shortest life, 30–40 years at present. It is also the fuel with the greatest flexibility in its applications and the one transported most easily. Can you think of ways in which it can be made available more cheaply in energy-poor developing countries?
4   World oil trade. Make a study of the flows of oil as given in table B. You may be able to map the origins of oil for selected countries (named in the top row) or map the location of principal exporters. Think about the best ways of representing these data cartographically.

Table B World oil trade in millions of tonnes moved

Importers / Exporters		Africa	USA	Brazil	India	Japan	South Korea	Singapore	Belgium	Czechoslovakia	France	GDR	GFR	Italy	Spain
Saudi Arabia	450	8	56	16	2	71	14	20	12		44		20	33	15
USSR	120	1			3				1	18	5	19	1	5	1
United Arab Emirates	71	7	4	1	1	26	1	2	1		7			2	3
Venezuela	67	1	8	4		2			1		2		1	4	3
Nigeria	64	2	31	3		1			1		6		5		1
Mexico	57		24	2		4					3				8
UK	51		15			1					3		16		
Libya	51		14	1							1		10	12	4
Indonesia	50		12	1		26					1				
Iran	41	11			2	7		4			1		2	3	5
Kuwait	41	1		1		12	5	1	1		3		1	1	1
Iraq	34	1		7	7	3		3			5	1		8	2
Algeria	24		11			2					2		4	3	2
Norway	20		5								3		3		
Qatar	19		2	1		7									
Oman	16		1			8									
China	14			1		9							2	2	1
World total	1,285														

Source: United Nations, *Energy Statistics Yearbook* (1982), New York, United Nations.

Chapter 5

1   Conservation. How durable is the natural environment? How can it be
    kept from destruction as increasing numbers of humans 'graze' on it? Is
    there a case for rationing the number of humans in different parts of the
    world as a farmer would control his livestock according to the
    availability of fodder for them?
2   Pollution. We now have the power to wipe out all life on this planet.
    Nuclear war, locally or globally? What would the consequences be?
    Other wars?
3   Physical overcrowding, especially in big cities (Mexico City, São Paulo).

Bibliography

Data bases

Natural resources

BP Statistical Review of World Energy (1985) London, The British Petroleum Company.

Brown, L.R. (1978) 'The worldwide loss of cropland', *Worldwatch Paper 24*, Washington DC, Worldwatch Institute.

Crowson, P. and Francis, S. (1977) *Non-Fuel Minerals and Foreign Policy Data Base*, London, Royal Institute of International Affairs.

Eckholm, E. (1975) 'The other energy crisis: firewood', *Worldwatch Paper 1*, Washington DC, Worldwatch Institute.

Mineral Facts and Problems (1980 edition), Washington DC, Bureau of Mines Bulletin 671.

United Nations, *Energy Statistics Yearbook*, New York, United Nations.

Production

Food and Agriculture Organization, *Production Yearbook* and *Trade Yearbook*, Rome.

United Nations, *Statistical Yearbook*, New York, United Nations.

World Bank, annual *World Development Report*, Washington DC.

Population

Population Reference Bureau, Inc., 2213 M Street, Washington DC, 20037 USA, especially the yearly *World Population Data Sheet*.

United Nations, annual *Demographic Yearbook*, especially 1979 for historical data sets for all countries.

Trade

United Nations, *Yearbook of International Trade Statistics*, New York, United Nations.

Books

Allen, R. (1980) *How to Save the World. A Strategy for World Conservation*, London, Kogan Page International Union for Conservation of Nature and Natural Resources.

Barney, G.O. (Study Director) (1982) *The Global 2000 Report to the President*, Harmondsworth, Penguin Books.

Brandt Commission, The (1983) *Common Crisis North-South: Cooperation for Third World Recovery*, London, Pan Books.

Chisholm, M. (1982) *Modern World Development*, London, Hutchinson.

Cole, J.P. (1981) *The Development Gap*, Chichester, Wiley.

Cole, J.P. (1983) *Geography of World Affairs*, London, Butterworth.

Crow, B. and Thomas, A. (1984) *Third World Atlas*, Milton Keynes, Open University Press.

Dickenson, J.P. and others (1983) *A Geography of the Third World*, London, Methuen.

Eyre, S.R. (1978) *The Real Wealth of Nations*, London, Arnold.

Liu Zheng and others (1981) *China's Population: Problems and Prospects*, Beijing, New World Press.

Mabogunje, A.L. (1980) *The Development Process*, London, Hutchinson.

Mesarovic, M. and Pestel, E. (1975) *Mankind at the Turning Point*, London, Hutchinson.

Redclift, M. (1984) *Development and the Environmental Crisis*, London, Methuen.

Rostow, W.W. (1975) *How It All Began*, London, Methuen.

Rostow, W.W. (1960) *The Stages of Economic Growth*, Cambridge, Cambridge University Press.

Simon, J.L. and Kahn, H. (1984) *The Resourceful Earth*, Oxford, Blackwell.

Papers

Flower, A.R. (1978) 'World oil production', *Scientific American* 238 (3), 42–9.

Gold, T. and Stohr, S. (1980) 'The deep-earth-gas hypothesis', *Scientific American* 242 (6), 130–7.

Keyfitz, N. (1976) 'World resources and the world middle class', *Scientific American* 235 (1), 28–35.

Manners, G. (1981) 'Our planet's resources', *Geographical Journal* 147, 1–22.

Nef, J.U. (1977) 'An early energy crisis and its consequences', *Scientific American* 237 (5), 140–51.

Scientific American, September 1980, the whole number devoted to economic development.

Index